What Is a
Jewish Classicist?

Rubicon

Series editor: Thomas Harrison

This new series seeks to challenge and refresh the study of antiquity: to re-examine central texts and questions, to disrupt stale orthodoxies, to test and problematize the nature and limits of our disciplines, to champion new approaches and to respond to the latest developments in research and in our contemporary world. *Rubicon* breaks through barriers – to open up the history, literature and culture of the ancient world.

What Is a Jewish Classicist?

Essays on the Personal Voice and Disciplinary Politics

Simon Goldhill

BLOOMSBURY ACADEMIC
LONDON • NEW YORK • OXFORD • NEW DELHI • SYDNEY

BLOOMSBURY ACADEMIC
Bloomsbury Publishing Plc
50 Bedford Square, London, WC1B 3DP, UK
1385 Broadway, New York, NY 10018, USA
29 Earlsfort Terrace, Dublin 2, Ireland

BLOOMSBURY, BLOOMSBURY ACADEMIC and the Diana logo are trademarks
of Bloomsbury Publishing Plc

First published in Great Britain 2022

Cover design: Terry Woodley

A catalogue record for this book is available from the British Library.

A catalog record for this book is available from Library of Congress.

ISBN: HB: 978-1- 3503-2257-8
       PB: 978-1- 3503-2253-0
       ePDF: 978-1- 3503-2254-7
       eBook: 978-1- 3503-2255-4

Typeset by RefineCatch Limited, Bungay, Suffolk
Printed and bound in Great Britain

To find out more about our authors and books visit
www.bloomsbury.com and sign up for our newsletters.

Contents

Series Editor's Preface

How does the study of antiquity move forward? How does it progress? In one common model, the study of the past is figured as a process of the filling-in of gaps. ('This book fills a much-needed gap', Moses Hadas quipped in a well-known rejoinder.) Even if we accept that this is a process without end – that our object of study is like a jigsaw puzzle that will always defy completion – it is a model that is easily taken for granted. For one thing, it makes easy sense to the wider audiences for academic research. 'How can you say anything new about *that*?', I am asked incredulously. In response, talk of new discoveries provides a kind of trump card. But the model of gap-filling is also an easy refuge for scholars of antiquity themselves. With the increased specialisation and compartmentalisation of our areas of study, and the imperatives of research assessment, tenure or promotion, there are ample pressures to find a comfortable niche that you can make your own, and to write footnote-heavy works that few will object to (or read in the first place).

Rubicon is founded in an alternative understanding of modern scholarship. Major new papyri, a coin hoard here, an inscription there: these can certainly re-orient our overall picture. Sometimes they can do more, and throw all the pieces of the jigsaw in the air. More often than not, however, change in understanding comes from other directions: from shifts in intellectual fashion, developments in other disciplines, or – underlying these – from the changed world in which we are operating. *Rubicon* starts from the position that, as scholars and readers, we are located in our particular times and places, shaped by our individual histories, and that the rules of the game of the study of antiquity – far from being timeless and immutable – have a history also. It sets out to understand and to interrogate these larger currents that impact on the study of antiquity, to engage with fundamental aspects of antiquity and our relationship with it.

Rubicon also sets out to break through the boundaries that too often confine and restrict our approaches: the boundaries between disciplines and scholarly approaches; between time periods; and between areas of study. The series encompasses – and moves between – the history, literature, languages, art and material culture of the ancient world (and anything else not covered within that list!), and the 'reception' of antiquity in later centuries. It seeks to draw on the insights of other disciplines and fields of study. The volumes in this series also range across the Mediterranean and Near Eastern worlds – and further afield. This is not a 'Classics' series, and no people or culture has an assumed primacy.

Finally, although all the volumes are informed by a deep expertise, they are not weighed down by it. 'If the love and knowledge of Greek literature ever die . . .,' wrote the Irish Hellenist E. R. Dodds in 1943, 'they will die of a suffocation arising from its exponents' industry'. The title of this series, *Rubicon*, is not *quite* an invitation to march on Rome, or to dismantle the structures and institutions of our disciplines. It does, however, represent a challenge: to question the assumptions and orthodoxies of our fields; to open up new areas of study, new vistas; and, above all, to *take risks*.

Thomas Harrison
St Andrews

Introduction: Fitting in

Every year, King's College, Cambridge, where I work, holds a dinner for its newly arrived first-year students. It has done so for centuries. As a Fellow, I sit with the new classicists whom I am going to teach for the next three years (or more). It is always a slightly nervy, even febrile occasion, as the new students, in the imposing Hogwarts-esque surroundings, are faced with unfamiliar classmates for the first time, over a dinner more formal than almost everyone is used to – lots of glasses and cutlery, a menu, food and wine served by staff – and they are all trying out their role as Cambridge students for the first time in Cambridge, in a mixture of performed insouciance, over-excitement and nervous apprehension (or just resistance). One year, the girl sitting next to me, turned and asked why I was not eating meat as she and the others around her were. I might have said that I was a vegetarian – easy option, often taken – but I replied that I was Jewish and ate only kosher meat. 'Oh,' she said, surprised, 'I didn't know you could be Jewish and English.'

She had, she went on, actually never met a Jew. Now, this scenario may seem just flabbergasting, if not ridiculous, or strike you as a sign of desperate parochialism (all too English?). But this girl turned out to be a very accomplished young woman, indeed, who graduated in classics with a double first, the very highest possible degree, and then quickly retrained in science and qualified as a medical doctor, again with the highest possible grades. You could see her comment as no more than a nervous blurt (her filters were never that strong). It certainly didn't stop us from having productive and supportive interactions in and out of class over the next ten years. But her comment completely threw me and consequently stuck in my mind. 'How,' I asked myself, 'could you grow up in the south of England and never meet a Jew?'; 'How could you think Jewishness was incompatible with Englishness?' If you come from New York, as my wife does, it was an even more baffling scenario, though she, too, could turn it happily into a sniffy exile's gibe about The Brits.

The exchange did leave the student and me both looking oddly at each other, as we tried to make sense of our mutual surprise. But it actually led to a far more interesting discussion than the usual conversations on such a potentially awkward occasion: I probed about her home life; she asked why and how I was a Jew. I had something to report when I went home later. The conversation also captured one of the strange dynamics of working in a university. For the girl, this was one step in the transformative time of being a student: not just learning a subject, but also learning who you want to be, and who others are – people outside your familiar and familial circles. For me, teacher, academic, who was going to spend an hour or more every week of term over the next few years with her, it was also a first step in participating in such an educational process. But the exchange was also discomforting for me, because at the very time I was meant to be welcoming the student into the community, I was being asked to face my own alterity in her eyes. The dialogue was, I suppose, a tiny, shared drama about fitting in.

The statement, 'I didn't know you could be Jewish and English,' however parochially naive it may sound at first, could easily be translated into a familiar, motivated political hostility, and not just in England, of course. When John Kennedy ran for President of the United States of America, his opponents played up what they declared to be his dual and thus fractured loyalty as a Roman Catholic. Would the Pope be giving him instructions on policy? The same rhetoric was not used against Joe Biden only because other hostile suggestions of conflicted loyalties were mobilized – and the toxic connection between politics and religion had moved to other battlegrounds. Every immigrant who raises a challenging question about his new host country has heard the sneering rejoinder, 'If you don't like it here, go home,' as if the place that has been fled, that other place, must be the real home of a stranger. The English politician, Norman Tebbit, became a byword for this sneering racism within the Conservative Party when he accused British Asians of not being sufficiently integrated if they supported the Indian or Pakistani cricket team: you could not be properly English, it seems, unless you cheered loudly for the home team. The so-called 'Tebbit Test' was designed to fail and thus stigmatize immigrants and their descendants: to make their unreliability visible. Jeremy Corbyn, with a cloth-ear for his own prejudice, reckoned Jews, however long they had been in the country, did not get English irony. The politics of identity has all too often rested on this sort of demand for purity: a single, simple label, which identifies and excludes, rhetorically, institutionally, aggressively.

Has there ever been a politics of identity that is not mired in such oversimplification, hostility or blithe misrecognition? Nobody is *just* English, *just* Black, *just* Muslim, *just* a woman, *just* queer … But the pressure of self-assertion, prejudice and oppression repeatedly produces a polarizing rhetoric that strives – often too successfully, always violently – to enforce such distinctions – to proclaim and defend the ideals of purity, especially when faced with the awkward evidence of intersectionality (or just the transgression of mixing). Many are made to feel *just* … Black, Muslim, queer and so forth, in the hostile eyes of others. 'That time and that time and that time the outside blistered the inside of you, words, outmanoeuvred years, had you in a chokehold, every part roughed up, the eyes dripping,' in Claudia Rankine's excruciating words.[1] Identity is also *inflicted*.

Here's a story that stopped me in my tracks, though. Faraj Alnasser, a young Syrian man, regained consciousness in Dover to find himself surrounded by police and interpreters. He had crossed the Channel from Dunkirk in a refrigerated lorry: of the fourteen people locked in the back, only two survived; he was dragged, unconscious, from among the frozen bodies of his travelling companions. Faraj had left Syria when he was fifteen because of the civil war, and moved with his family to Cairo. He had fled Cairo for Turkey on his own at sixteen. Faraj is gay, and comes from a committedly Muslim family, where he had experienced violence and denigration even before he came out. In Turkey, he was unable either to get an education or to regularize his status, so after a year of living on the streets or in temporary jobs where he could sleep on the floor, he started his trek across Europe. After a precarious overloaded boat ride to Greece, he walked through Greece, Macedonia and onwards north. In Hungary, he was thrown into prison for ten days for being a refugee, stripped naked and, in deliberate insult, offered only pork to eat. They stamped his papers and warned him that if he was found in Hungary again, he would be imprisoned automatically for three years. Nonetheless, he tried to cross the country again – the only route – and, threatened by an armed policeman, tripped him up, grabbed his gun, and ran through the woods to escape. (He threw the gun into the trees.) He made his way to Germany and on to France – on foot – and ended in the 'jungle' at Dunkirk, where he spent every night in terrified tears, threatened by organized crime, traffickers and desperate refugees. When he awoke in Dover, the English policeman was gentle and told him through an

---

[1]Rankine (2015: 156).

interpreter that he was safe – Faraj spoke no English at that point. The policeman then went through his list of questions: 'Name?' 'Where are you from?' 'What colour are you?' This last question baffled Faraj. It was asked again. 'I am *this* colour,' he said, holding his arm up. The enquiry made no sense to him: why couldn't the policeman *see* what colour he was? Why did the policeman ask at all? In his community in Syria, a mix of country and city people, but all Muslims, colour was not a defining characteristic. It was simply not a marker of identity. Why was *this* one of the first questions to ask a refugee?

Now, four years on, secure, speaking English well, and working as a chef (though without having received adequate support from the government to integrate into British life), Faraj can laugh about this part of his harrowing story, and grins, 'Maybe I should have said olive.' Well, it is a colour, but, of course, not the sort of answer the policeman was looking for. This whole traumatic story only gradually emerged over the four years that Faraj has lived in our house, learned enough English to express himself, and built enough security, trust and confidence to tell his story fully and allow his story to be told. (After what happened to Jewish refugee families in the Second World War, there was no choice for us when offered the opportunity to take Faraj into our house and give him his chance – the necessary *care*.) It is, to my mind, truly remarkable that any young man can emerge from such a journey smiling, trusting and engagingly happy. But what fascinates me, too, about the story is the clash of expectations between the policeman and the refugee. In this case, the police were polite and careful in their treatment of a stowaway; asylum was achieved moderately quickly from the Home Office since Faraj had kept detailed and dated records of his journey across Europe. But the policeman had been trained in what identity meant – and colour was crucial. For Faraj, colour *as a category* simply did not signify meaningfully in such a political situation. To be brought into the community was to find himself situated, categorized, interpellated in an incomprehensible and distorting manner. The exchange was a really serious drama of fitting in.

This story of official racial recognition through colour has a decent ending. Most don't. Of all the proclaimed and buttressed purities of identity, racial purity has been perhaps the most damagingly incoherent, historically, and still is today. It is impossible – or should be impossible – to study the categories which immigration regulations enshrine, or the laws of racial mixing, or the brutal practices of racial violence, without both being horrified by human cruelty and being shocked at humanity's desperate inability to accommodate difference.[2] Far worse still is to experience the force of such cruelty and such conceptual shackles. It is, consequently, all the harder to acknowledge and respect the contingencies, shifting relational matrices and temporal developments of a person's identity (or identities): the multiple dynamics of positionality. But to do so, productively, attentively, carefully, is to resist the grimly instrumental, oversimplifying politics of identity that have shaped so much social conflict. And there is a political purchase in that refusal.

The history of exclusion and privilege associated with classics, made more visible by the contemporary politics of identity, has produced a crisis within the discipline of classics, and the essays in this book were written as an engagement with this crisis – an

---

[2] All the footnotes in this book are designedly selective, in line with its essay format. This one most obviously so: the bibliography on historical and contemporary racial discrimination and violence is huge and growing. But, for a hopelessly tiny group of paired exemplary texts that have influenced me, see for now (more later in the chapters), on immigration policy: Molina (2014) and Perlman (2018; with the studies cited in n. 5); more generally, Gilroy (1987 and 1993); on witnessing, Felman and Laub (1992) and Wood (2009); on law, Williams (1991) and Alexander (2010); and on the university, Ahmed (2012) and Wilder (2013). Novels, memoirs, films and poetry have contributed hugely to the recognition and acknowledgement of racial violence: Padilla Peralta (2015) and Allen (2017), looking back, for example, to Wideman (1984), are in a long line ...

intervention. But it is a specific version of my student's question that echoes through this book: What is a Jewish classicist? To ask this question is not to displace other narratives of cultural disparagement, passing or suffering. Being Jewish may be less likely now than in the past to raise the antipathy of the institutional gatekeepers of the discipline, but systemic prejudice against others remains pervasive and pernicious. (There is enough prejudice to go round, and competitive narratives of victimhood are a particularly unproductive distraction from collaborative instrumental discussion – and action towards change.)[3] Rather, my question is precisely to wonder about the limits and boundaries of the discussion of cultural identity and classics. It should be obvious that in recent years there have been few bars to Jews entering and making a successful career in the discipline of classics (though forms of anti-Semitism certainly continue in the field as they do, more violently, throughout society); it should be equally obvious that before and immediately after the Second World War, this was not the case: before 1930, only one Jew was tenured in a classics department in America – and he entered an administrative role very quickly – a pattern of exclusion mirrored across Europe, too; many years after the war, Moses Hadas, who from his post in New York had himself done so much to popularize classics, still warned the young Seth Schein not to enter the discipline because of its ingrained anti-Semitism.[4] One reason why the question, 'What is a Jewish classicist?' interests me is this *changing* historical narrative – what has been discussed recently in America under the polemical title of 'how Jews became white' (following the discussion of how the Irish, too, became white, or Italians claimed their status as white) – stories predicated on the continuing crushing of Blackness at the bottom of

---

[3]See Baldwin ([1967] 1969) with Gordon (2015), Glaude (2021) and Eddo-Lodge (2017).
[4]For details and sources, see Chapter 2.

the hierarchy, a motivational factor in the current debates about access to the discipline.[5] How, and how much, is being a Jewish classicist a question of fitting in? It is because there is such contentiousness about when and how Jewishness matters in questions of politics and identity that Jewishness has become something of a conundrum even and especially for critical race theory, which has not always integrated religion into its theoretical perspectives.[6] The Jewish question, it seems, is harder to shelve than it might have been hoped. How Jews fit into the debate on the politics of identity, then, provides one – and only one – focus for what follows.

These essays are also about the discipline of classics and the idea of the classical tradition. These are two interlinked ideas. On the one hand, the history of disciplines finds a paradigm in classics. The shape of the discipline – what subjects it includes, what students it allows, encourages, rewards, who it employs, what methodologies it develops – requires institutional as well as intellectual narratives of explanation. How classics relates to anthropology, theology, literary studies, history and so forth, articulates its place in the modern university.[7] To understand the discipline's current travails, such histories are necessary, and provide a framework for my discussion, which aims to contribute to the self-understanding of classics and classicists. The current political debates about classics as a discipline are particularly heated, however, because of the history of privilege and exclusion associated especially with classics from the nineteenth-century

---

[5]Brodkin (1998), Guglielmo (2003), Roedigger (2005), Goldstein (2006) and Treitler (2013); with Ignatiev (1995), and more journalistically and amusingly Baddiel (2021).
[6]Salaymeh and Lavi (2021). On critical race theory and classics, see McCoskey (2012). It is shocking that as this is being written, it is reported that some states in America are trying to ban the teaching of critical race theory, much as both Poland and Hungary have passed laws to restrict research which might criticize a partisan political agenda.
[7]Zon and Lightman, eds (2019).

redesign of the universities, the disciplines and the world order (Thomas Hardy's novel, *Jude the Obscure*, 1895, is already a passionate comment on classics as a gatekeeper to privilege). Can admission to classics militate successfully against society's continuing and destructive patterns of social exclusion and disadvantage? That is the core of the current debate. On the other hand, the history of the discipline is constantly implicated in what gets called the 'classical tradition'. The phrase, 'classical tradition', is popular only surprisingly late in the long history of the engagement with the classical past, and only when such a tradition is perceived to be under severe threat.[8] But how Western societies have made the antiquity of Greece and Rome a privileged past has become a subject of growing passion in contemporary academia.[9] This book asks rather what role the rhetoric of tradition has played and continues to play in the self-description of the discipline, and what the institutional and conceptual consequences of this rhetoric are. How admission – both of people and ideas – to the discipline is regulated, and how modernity constructs its sense of tradition, are interlinked and pressing questions of fitting in. Because these questions are integral to how we think about the discipline and how it should change, they are worth answering well – with richness, nuance and purposiveness.

It will not have escaped your notice that the question, 'What is a Jewish classicist?' is being asked here by a Jewish classicist. The third concern – and the first chapter – of this book asks how the personal voice can and should be mobilized in an academic context. What one Edwardian critic rather wonderfully called 'autobiografiction' has (again) become a particularly fertile mode of contemporary prose

---

[8]Kallendorf (2010: 1–2) and Ziolkowski (2010) – who cite the importance of Highet (1949) – whose dismissive attitude to Jews, in particular, is noted in Chapter 2, pp. 81, 86.
[9]My own contributions in Goldhill (2002, 2011, 2013).

(Karl-Ove Knausgaard's *My Struggle* and Rachel Cusk's *Outline* trilogy are particularly brilliant examples).[10] The theory of autobiographical narrative has also been the subject of superb interventions by critics, as has the role of the personal voice, especially in feminist theory. Yet, there is all too often something of a gap between such carefully poised, self-reflexive and self-aware prose, on the one hand, and the debates on the politics of identity, on the other. When talking about oneself, it is good to remember Oliver Cromwell's injunction to the Church of Scotland, 'I beseech you, in the bowels of Christ, think it possible that *you may be mistaken*' – or as Freud taught, self-knowledge can only be hard-won, and the stories we do tell of our self are – in all senses – self-serving (and, we might add, shifty and self-deceptive). Yet, the situatedness of the scholar requires analysis, and any classicist worth her salt will recognize that the unexamined life is not worth living. As academics, we are constantly asked to provide a brief biography, which, like Caesar's *Gallic Wars*, is always written in the third-person: 'Simon Goldhill is a professor of Greek at the University of Cambridge. He . . .' To write in the first-person singular is a much harder task. Yet, how can the politics of identity be discussed without acknowledging a first-person narrative?

Classicists write and read biographies of other classicists and autobiographies: the history of the discipline – and their own place in it – has been a long-lasting fascination for generations of classicists. Narcissistic? Another sign of a proclaimed tradition misrecognizing its own ideology? Just good gossip? There are certainly many volumes from the nineteenth century onwards that read these days rather too much like self-congratulatory narratives of privilege and institutional triumph, or which, like Kenneth Dover's *Marginal Comment*, mistake self-exposure for self-reflection. But let's be generous and suppose that

---

[10]Saunders (2010).

this genre is following the biblical injunction to, 'Remember the days of old; consider the years long past. Ask your father, and he will tell you, your elders, and they will inform you' – a recognition, that is, of how finding a place in a disciplinary history is a shared enterprise for any classicist. And, for sure, the circulation of such biographical material is also a way of projecting and promoting a normative image of how to be a classicist – and thus now, too, a way of calibrating the misrecognitions, complicities and values that indicate the intergenerational and transitional trajectory of the contemporary discipline. (The life-writing of the past is also a portal to the stresses and struggles of the discipline in those times. A continually contentious discipline ...) To ask, as I have, about the history of the discipline and to ask about the personal voice are, then, significantly interconnected and mutually implicative questions of fitting in. But this book is most certainly *not* an autobiography. It uses personal anecdotes – mine and others – to give a perspective *from within* of how the field has changed, is changing and needs to change, *and* how this can be productively discussed. How the field has been shaped and needs to transform matters, personally, to every classicist, I hope. This is not a third-person story, for any of us. And it should be a story with dialogue, a conversation.

The three essays that make up this volume are linked by these three connected questions, then. How does the contemporary anxiety about the politics of identity in classics, expressed most pointedly around race, deal with Jewishness? How does the disciplinary formation of classics and its sense of tradition inform that first question and the integral issue of inclusion and exclusion? How are we to write in the first-person singular about becoming and being a classicist?

There is also a trajectory of argument that runs through the three essays which is worth outlining here. I begin with the question of personal voice and how the positionality of the scholar articulates a relation to the discipline and to their own work within it. It seems to me that much of the fuss over the politics of identity in classics is fuelled by a lack of self-reflectiveness about such self-implication, conjoined with an unhealthy degree of self-righteousness: it is *hard* – and *should* be hard – to write decently about oneself, and one's own politicized engagement – as writers from Augustine to Freud have demonstrated so engagingly, both in theory and practice. There is a politics in acknowledging and recognizing this difficulty, a politics that stands against the violence of slogans and the violence of brutal oversimplification of what persons are, the violence demanded by racism and other forms of extreme politics.

The second chapter, that gives the book its title, views the story of the discipline and its treatment of the specific question of Jewishness through what we could call a sociological or anthropological lens. This lens is not so much a statistical accounting nor a disciplinary history of the sort so tellingly constructed by, say, Christopher Stray or earlier by Arnaldo Momigliano, but an account that draws on the first chapter's question of the personal voice to collect and analyse the personal stories of a group of classicists working in the field, set against the history of the exclusion and gradual inclusion of those identified as Jews within the academy, specifically in departments of classical study. It is fascinating to reflect on how a question which seemed so burning between around 1850 to 1950 – the so-called 'Jewish Question' – has been muted in current discussions of race and entitlement within the discipline – and what this can tell us about historical self-awareness of scholarship as well as changing social patterns of privilege.

The final chapter turns towards the internal working of the discipline in a different way. There is no department of classics that is not deeply involved with the business of translation. Every classicist has to learn at some level that access to antiquity is gained through the languages of Greece and Rome (alongside material culture in its multiple forms).

Translation classes are, for most departments, the bread and butter of the field. Yet, even at this most basic sense of translation, here, too, politics can flair into public brouhaha. As I write, the American press has been galvanized by news that Princeton University – already embroiled in a string of public rows about its Department of Classics – is allowing students to complete a major in Classics without a language requirement. It would be easy to dismiss it all as no more than a storm in a teacup, or, rather, as an alibi for a wider and deeply unpleasant – in motivation and personality – culture war. But there is a long history which shows how much is at stake specifically in translation. We could start with the Renaissance's rediscovery of the Greek texts of Scripture, and the traumatic effects of their consequent re-translation into Latin and then vernacular languages, that fuelled the Reformation; we could think of the power of the translation of the King James Bible, a lasting impact on literary and spoken English; we could add the long and politically transformative rows about who knows Greek and what knowledge of Greek meant in Victorian education for Victorian society, a commitment to broadening access to education that is still being demanded. *Translatio*, indeed, is at the very heart of why classicism matters. At one level, any study of antiquity is about how one culture can be appropriated, redrafted, understood by another – translated. At another, the politics of international power has repeatedly been expressed as *translatio imperii* or *translatio scientiae* – the transfer of power and the transfer of knowledge integral to imperial projects. As a schoolboy, I was told by my teachers the *ben trovato* story of Charles Napier, the English commander fighting in India in the 1840s, who sent back to London the single word message *peccavi* – which he knew would be understood as an announcement of his victory – 'I have Sindh' – he had conquered the province. This story was told to us boys as a witty triumph of classical learning – we were all *in the know* that *peccavi* meant 'I have sinned' – but now I hear it as the continuing circulation of

a link between the schoolroom education into a world view and its
imperial enactment on the world stage. Translation as a symbol of
translatio imperii. At a further level, translation also looks towards the
transformation of the self that classics promises – the *Bildung* that
educates a person into a civilized citizen. ('Bottom, thou art translated,'
as Shakespeare has it, his parody of a lover's transformation.) Translation
also links the technology of the subject of classics to the formation of
the classical scholar as a person. It is not by chance that Matthew
Arnold, great arbiter of culture for Victorian Britain, let on that he spent
his evening's relaxation translating poems from the Greek Anthology. It
was a knowing self-representation. This final chapter thus looks at the
discipline of classics through a central technology of the field, but in a
way that looks back to the personal engagement of classicists in their
scholarship. Translation studies has all too often passed over the cultural
history of translation.

Consequent and compelling issues of privilege, entitlement,
education, national and racial difference, career and age, all come up
inevitably and in due course. But, for now, I want to conclude this
introduction by noting that each of these essays was formulated in
sharp and collaborative conversations with friends and colleagues.
There is a long note *in loco* listing all who contributed to Chapter 2,
and a further note in Chapter 3 indicating those who offered me help
from their specific expertise, with special thanks there also to Richard
Armstrong for a long, wide-ranging and fun exchange. Other editorial
advice came from Tom Harrison, Josh Billings, Felix Budelmann,
Alexandra Lianeri, Patricia Rosenmeyer and Vered Lev Kanaan. Most
importantly, however, each chapter has been debated, tested and
refined repeatedly with particularly dear friends, whom I gratefully
name and thank here: Catherine Conybeare, Helen Morales,
Constanze Güthenke, Johanna Hanink.

1

The Personal Voice: Six Fragments of a Sentimental Education

And, oh!
The difference to me!
WILLIAM WORDSWORTH

If I am not what you say I am, you are not who you say you are.
JAMES BALDWIN

You are what Grammy Hall would call a real Jew.
Annie Hall in Woody Allen's *Annie Hall* (1977)

i Sleepless in Seattle

A few years ago, I was invited to speak at the Classics Department of the University of Washington at Seattle. The choice of invited speaker, in this particular programme, was delegated to the graduate students, who, under the terms of the programme, also invited me to an opening question-and-answer forum with them, scheduled for the evening before the formal lecture. This was an event around a table and over a bottle of wine (my stipulation), and the first question – alas, I do not now remember the graduate student's name – was brilliantly provocative, a great way to open such an intimate occasion: 'What do you most dislike about the field of classics?' In my panicked mind, I immediately stumbled through a tumble of thoughts – the nasty senior academics who had tried to block my research when I was starting out, the horrid reviews I had received, the lack of intellectual generosity and openness of some scholars, the negative conservatism that sometimes marred the field, its unwillingness to lead the humanities as it had so often done in the past – and I tried, with a jangly mixture of personal anecdotes, verging on the narcissistic, and some rather bland general political points about exclusion and openness, to hazard an answer. It wasn't very coherent or satisfying – to me, or, I suspect, them – and left me quite flustered. It has bugged me ever since, and I have occasionally imagined better answers, without quite cracking it. This essay is my attempt to find a better answer to that smart graduate student's question, finally.

The unexamined discipline is not worth living in. When classicists of pretty well any level and in pretty well any institutional setting get together, complaints about the discipline flow easily enough. These complaints can grow not just into changes of intellectual perspective and understanding, but also into insistent political awareness and articulated moves toward change. Current debates about the curriculum and about access and diversity are part of a long history of what a discipline *must* do if it is to breathe and live – as well as speaking compellingly to today (as I will get to in Chapter 3). The place and practice of classics have been argued about since at least the Renaissance, often bitterly, sometimes murderously. It is not passionate caring about the discipline that is bad for the field, but the desire not to examine itself sharply. What left me flustered and sleepless in Seattle, however, was not just how best to engage with such disciplinary self-analysis. It was rather the place of the personal voice in such a process. What I heard upfront in the question was the invitation to begin an answer with 'I' and to frame it as a 'dislike' – not so much a political analysis as an emotional response. How far out on a limb was I prepared to go? What – I worried – did they want to know?

Imagine if the question had been, '*Who* do you most dislike in the discipline of classics?' Easier to answer, but immediately the question looks invidious at best, and, at worst, an invitation to rant in a self-centred way through a slew of personal hurts and insults (we all have them). Or perhaps to confess to an all-embracing love, like Mr Rodgers. Unconvincingly. But how to talk about the 'I' in terms of 'like' and 'dislike' *without* going into some such self-exposure? The question would not have felt answered if I had retreated behind the generalities of prosopography – we need to change the make-up of the field – or the blandness of curriculum talk – we need more theoretical awareness, or more work in late antiquity or ... For sure, such generalities are significantly motivated by, and experienced, as individual and personal narratives. They must be. But how are such personal narratives to be mobilized? Especially when I was invited as a professor from one of the grandest – most privileged – universities, to speak to a group of graduate students starting in the profession, I was fairly sure that any tale of early struggle, however instructive, would reek of *amour propre*, and any account of my current institutional work aimed at changing what I disliked, would smack of self-justification.

What's more, I was brought up as a scholar under two different competing trajectories – like Liber and Venus, *durus uterque deus*. On the one hand, I had been trained, as you would expect, to argue from evidence presented in a way that is disciplined (carefully chosen term, that), and either to resist or to mark carefully where judgement veered towards a personal opinion or a speculation. On the other hand, for many years, I had studied and absorbed theoretical discussions in classics and elsewhere about the personal voice. As a young academic, I had revelled in Jane Gallop's bravado expositions of how the personal and the professional intertwined; I deeply admire Sara Ahmed's analysis, based on her personal experience and curated anecdotal evidence, of institutional sluggishness about institutional racism and sexism.[1] I knew that it was impossible to talk about the field without talking about oneself – and how tricky a task that is.

I also knew that *where the voice is*, the voice that is personal, that speaks of the speaker as a person, cannot be located solely in explicit autobiography. It is also in the strategies of self-presentation that are projected by any writing, including silences. It is in the anticipation of reception that the exchanges of writing, teaching, talking embody. It is in the situatedness of the scholar, and the self-consciousness, admitted or denied but always performed, in speaking *from somewhere*.[2] Not just partiality, but, as Rita Felski insists, attachments.[3] The three essentials of successfully persuasive rhetoric, declared Demosthenes, who knew, are *hupokrisis, hupokrisis, hupokrisis*: 'self-presentation, self-presentation, self-presentation' (or 'delivery, delivery, delivery', if you prefer, a weak translation, which leaves out the essential aspect of *êthos*).[4] The desire for objectivity in the scholarly voice, with its corresponding terror of being judged subjective or, worse, emotional, creates academic prose, but also the academic person(a). This *êthos* of

---

[1] Gallop (1985, 1988, 1997) and Ahmed (2004, 2012, 2017). Hallett and Van Nortwick, eds (1997). The annotations to this chapter are designedly few and pointed.
[2] Haraway (1988) is seminal.
[3] Felski (2020).
[4] Plut. *Lives of the Ten Orators* 845a; see Hall (1995).

spectacular distance all too often makes it hard for academics even to express why and how they care about their subject: what is at stake in it for them, how they are implicated in their argument (or not). Even harder to do with sophistication, nuance and adequate self-awareness. My dear lamented friend Teresa Brennan, great feminist, psychoanalytic scholar and activist,[5] in witty despair diagnosed so many of her academic colleagues as 'sado-dispassionate' – they enacted the desire for objective distance by a form of perverse aggression, a wilful disregard of the personal. But you can't hide from the personal, only displace it. Good word, sado-dispassionate.

All this crippled my answer in Seattle. I was both hesitant about how to *place* my answer – politically, socially, intellectually (three different registers) – and, more distressingly, unable to disembarrass myself from the fact that, for all the theoretical understanding of the issues I reckoned I had, I still wasn't ready really to talk personally, not like this, not here, not now.

'I' *should* be a hard word to use. That's one challenge of this book, and, now, the specific challenge of this chapter. What I most dislike in ... discussions of the personal voice is when it is assumed, too readily, that the person and the voice are easy or self-evident categories. So, let me try to proceed otherwise.

ii Confession

I currently run a large-scale research project, funded by the Mellon Foundation, entitled 'Religious Diversity and the Secular University', which is focused on how the university, committed as it is to secular

---

[5]Brennan (1992); and Brennan (2004), posthumously published, and central to what I am writing.

values, can find a place for the religious commitments of the
communities from which it draws its students. One of the most
pressing contemporary problems not just for the academic community
but also – and more disturbingly – for the political order of the world,
is how to understand and respond to the current toxic combination
of religion and politics. It is a fundamental concern for the issue of
diversity, currently top of the political agenda in the institutions of
classics. How should the liberal ideal of a tolerant and mixed society
comprehend claims to exclusive and totalizing visions of truth, which
set themselves against such liberal ideals? We may recognize that
there is now, nationally and globally, a new and complex map, which
has more than one monotheism, and polytheism, competing alongside
secular standpoints. The challenge may be expressed like this: how
can we take account of theological difference without going to war for
belief? Quite simply, diversity in modern society cannot be adequately
broached without an engagement with religion.

The most immediate prompt for this project, however, is a piece of
British legislation, 'the "Prevent" strategy', which requires teachers at
all levels of the educational system to report to the authorities any
student they believe to be at risk of radicalization. It is a strange shift
in discourse. For many years, to be radical – a radical new idea, a
radical breakthrough – was a positive term in academia: now, the
government and press declare, it is to be taken as negative and
dangerous. Critics have stressed how damaging the breakdown of
trust between students and teachers, provoked by such a policy, is,
and, further, how naïve its view of extremism appears. Prevent, what's
more, seems aimed specifically at the Muslim community: in the
media, 'radical Muslim', as a phrase, is rarely paralleled by 'radical
Christian', 'radical Jew', 'radical racist' (let alone 'radical atheist'). It is a
striking fact, therefore, taken from the most recent figures, that more
than 50 per cent of referrals for radicalization have named white

supremacists. Our project hopes to develop a better policy or at least a better understanding of diversity than is evident in Prevent.

As part of the historical background to the issue, the project has run a series of international workshops on how particular disciplines in the university have dealt with religion. (For classicists, the separation of our field from theology is a fundamental vector in the self-representation of our own modernity.)[6] In our workshop on anthropology, one session started from a seminal book, Robert Orsi's, *The Madonna of 115th Street: Faith and Community in Italian Harlem, 1880–1950*, and the three prefaces to its three editions, which trace different responses of the author to his own project.[7] At one point, I asked the anthropologist who opened the discussion, whether Orsi was himself a Catholic. The anthropologist immediately responded in shocked tones, 'You can't ask that!' The discussion turned – inevitably – to why the religious beliefs or background of an academic should be felt to be a taboo subject, when gender, class, race, privilege, educational background have become standard forms of evaluating the positionality of a scholar. The confessional mode has become a trope of modern academia, hilariously parodied in Gary Shteyngart's memoir, *Little Failure*, where he describes how his social standing as a student at university changed for the better when he learned to begin any intervention in the class with, 'As an immigrant . . .'[8] The 'As a,' as he calls this trope, is the mark of the claim to personal authority, the personal voice at its most categorical, least individual. What can be a necessary, politically instrumental demand for recognition can also be trivialized into clumsy and unreflective self-assertion.[9] Yet, religion has an especially quiet place in such confessional

---

[6]Conybeare and Goldhill (2020).
[7]Orsi ([1985] 2010) contains the three prefaces.
[8]Shteyngart (2014: 255).
[9]This trope is discussed further below, on pp. 36–7, 89.

modes, despite the long history of confession as a religious term. Why has religious, confessional commitment not become a standard of academic confession?

The professionalization of the disciplines, including classics, of course, from the nineteenth century onwards, constructs a separation of public, professional values and private, domestic life. It is well known that one response of liberal democracy towards religion is to assert precisely that religion is a matter of private life, which should not be for the state to regulate, either to foster or to oppress – incisively studied recently by Cécile Laborde.[10] The separation of church and state is a fast-held tenet of the American way of life (however much Jesus is brought into politics these days); British politicians happily demand that religious leaders should not comment on politics; the French celebrate the nation's *laïcité*. Religion should be private. The personal voice, that is, carefully negotiates the private, not always coherently. What privacies does the personal maintain? It is politically *invasive* to ask about a colleague's religion. But there is a second reason, too. The secularization of the university – again, a process started in the nineteenth century – is fundamental to its modernity. At its most basic, any historical explanation that turns to Providence – God's hand – to explain causality is properly rejected and thoroughly despised. Embarrassment or dismissiveness of such explanations is even retrojected into antiquity, especially where historiography is concerned. Religious confession in the secular university is likely therefore to appear as a perversity, an embarrassment. (Universities that remain religious foundations negotiate such difficulties differently.) Like emotion, religious commitment raises concerns about objectivity. To ask whether Orsi was a Catholic immediately sounded to the anthropologist as if I was impugning Orsi's objectivity as a scholar, the value of his research – to suggest that he was

---

[10]Laborde (2017); see also Scott (2018), Mahmood (2015), Taylor (2007) and Asad (2003).

too much of a participant and not enough of an observer. To admit a *religious* personal voice would be immediately to raise suspicions, unless, perhaps, it was a story of lapsed or rejected religion, itself a popular genre from the nineteenth century that is still going strong.

It is not so easy to separate scholarly discourse from the religious, however. (Stories of rejected religion are modelled on conversion narratives . . .) The very word 'religion' marks out a modern religious category (as Brent Nongbri, and, differently, Carlin Barton and Daniel Boyarin have argued at length for antiquity)[11] – but it has proved difficult for everyone, including me, to talk about the relations of humans and gods or cosmology without reverting to that useful if anachronistic vocabulary for the ordering of things. The practice of close reading, nowadays endemic to classics, has its genealogy in specifically Protestant polemics, as does so much of modern thinking about the dangers of erotic visuality.[12] More specifically, consider this example, which stopped me in my tracks, taken from a recent, sophisticated book of literary criticism. Psalm 18 (19) describes the sun coming 'forth like a bridegroom from his chamber, and rejoices in running the race, like a giant; his coming forth is from the height of the sky. His circuit is to the height of it.' Ambrose, writing his Latin hymns in the fourth century, understands this image allegorically as referring to Jesus. Brian Dunkle, writing about Ambrose, comments, 'The Christological reading of the Psalms . . . does not compromise their integrity as texts about the Lord of the Old Testament.' Thus, he concludes, 'Ambrose retains a plain interpretation of the texts even as he offers a Christological or allegorical interpretation for his particular catechetical ends.'[13] When an image of the sun from several hundred

---

[11]Nongbri (2013) and Barton and Boyarin (2016); also Boyarin (2018) and Goldhill (2020: 149–93).
[12]Conybeare and Goldhill, eds (2020) and Steiner (1996).

years before the birth of Jesus is read as the figure of Jesus, how can 'the integrity' of a text be said to remain *uncompromised*? How can the 'plain interpretation' of a text about the sun be reconciled with a Christological – a supersessionist – interpretation? As if using the term, 'Old Testament', itself rather than 'Hebrew Bible' is not already fully complicit with this supersessionist ideology. Brian Dunkle – and this is, I repeat, in many ways a sophisticated and insightful book – signs himself on its cover as 'Brian Dunkle, SJ' – Society of Jesus, that is, he is a Jesuit priest. He announces his religious affiliation; and his interpretation is fully in line with such a commitment. It is precisely a *compromised* reading. His personal faith informs and fills his critical voice.

When I was commissioned to write this essay, it was suggested I should talk about a specific text and my affective response to it. Since I was working on a book about the invention of Christian time in late antiquity alongside the project on religious diversity and the secular university, I immediately offered to choose a religious text. It seemed to me that this would be an area of maximum difficulty. On the one hand, classical courses in the modern university, to speak generally, tend not to include the most influential texts from the period and culture they work on, if religion is involved: Hellenistic history marches on without the Septuagint; to work on Philo, the most prolific extant 'late Hellenistic' writer, will guarantee scholarly marginalization;[14] the Augustan literature course proceeds without the Gospels or the letters of Paul. Prudentius is discussed in relation to Virgil and Horace but not Ambrose, though it is Ambrose's hymns that are still sung in liturgy, daily. Jerome's Latin translation of the

---

[13]Dunkle (2016: 125).

[14]'Late Hellenistic' in the sense of Konig and Wiater, eds (forthcoming), who duly omit Philo.

Bible – the one piece of Latin that for centuries every literate European could be expected to have encountered – is resolutely ignored. It would make for a hilarious parody if it were not miserably true that the new *Cambridge Greek Lexicon*, edited by my colleague James Diggle in 2021, does not include Philo, Josephus, the Septuagint or Paul as source texts (guess what they have in common . . . they are all written by Jews), although the Septuagint and Paul have a very strong case to be two of the most influential Greek texts ever written. On the other hand, such religious texts demand a personal, affective response: they are designed to transform the reader, emotionally as well as intellectually. The genres of Greek literature have always written a reader response into themselves: the *Odyssey*'s dramatized scenes of listening to a bardic performance, or the chorus of tragedy's horrified response to what it witnesses, are paradigms, which have informed critical analysis from Plato's *Ion* and Aristotle's *Poetics*, onwards. But while the affective response to Greek literature is a familiar subject and performance of literary criticism, it is hard to point to exemplary models of classicists who have responded thus to the religious texts of antiquity, Christian or not, even with Augustine's *Confessions*, the greatest of self-representing, self-examining texts. The affective and the personal turn in classics – unlike in Victorian or earlier European literature – has turned its back on the religious.

I did therefore imagine that I might spend time – as I have a good deal recently – working through a paragraph of Augustine's *Confessions*, always a transformative experience, in my experience. But a more pressing politicized anger took over. It is perhaps no surprise that the Gospels and Paul have their attacks on Jews as a group. Nor is it still a shock that as Christianity became a recognized cult rather than a small separatist group of Jews, it needed to define itself more aggressively in a triangulated fashion against both the dominant culture of the Roman or Greek authorities and the Jewish community. It does not make the anti-Jewish literature, even Justin Martyr, any more pleasant to read. What finally angered me enough to write, however, was actually the sophisticated intellectual response to later Christian anti-Jewish polemics.[15] It has become a standard understanding of such literature – one I share – that much Christian anti-Jewish polemic is a mask for internal contentiousness within the Church, attacking other Christian groups, and using familiar tropes of disparagement to do so – stubborn, stiff-necked, law-bound, rejection of the faith and so forth. '"Jew" functioned as a negative code-word within purely Christian internal debate.'[16] What angered me is the implication that somehow this made the anti-Judaism acceptable, explainable, ignorable. It is not really *Jews* being attacked in anti-Jewish screeds. There is too long a history of specific murderous violence based on such attitudes, on the one hand, and an equally long tradition, still bitterly evident in modern Britain and elsewhere, of masking anti-Judaism in claims really to be talking about something else. Really.

Anger is the affect that is prompted by racism and sexism: as Aristotle stated most clearly, a just person *must* be angry. Anger at injustice prompts the desire for change. The scholarly calm in determining that the violent, hateful words of anti-Jewish attacks are not really about Jews – as if therefore they had no instrumental impact on the treatment of Jews – flabbergasts and then enrages me, I confess, as does the easy supersessionism of 'AD' and the 'Old Testament', religious dominance masked as secular 'ease of reference'. With

---

[15]The best introduction with full bibliography is Frederiksen and Ishai (2006); on the unique position of Augustine, see Frederiksen (2008).
[16]Frederiksen and Ishai (2006: 984). See Wilken (1983) and McLennan (1990); and for a full bibliography and discussion, see Mayer (2019). There are, of course, exceptions: Stroumsa (1996), Drake (2013) and Mayer (2019), who lists other examples.

response comes responsibility. Just as sexism and racism in comedy are never just joking, but have a social effect, so, too, scholarly indifference to the past's instrumentality is not just objectivity but a refusal of responsibility. Well, this time it's personal.

iii A real Jew

My parents, of blessed memory, came of age during the Second World War, and made a life for themselves and their family in London, moving from poverty to financial security, with my father, in particular, winning scholarships to private school and then university, before and after the war, in which he was wounded twice, and saved by the French resistance, who operated on his wounds, in a cellar, with calvados as anaesthetic and antiseptic. My parents in serious discussion, even at home, would never say the word 'Jew' without lowering their voices. After the war, my father had worked as an anti-fascist infiltrator in violent fascist groups, where he had to conceal his religious background, for his life. He was forced to live some time in hiding after being outed. Both my parents knew what was at stake in passing. And let their children know, too. Even in raucous humour among friends, the word Jew was rare. Jewish jokes usually talk about Manny or Solly or Mrs Cohen. Jokes that have 'a Jew' in them usually come from somewhere else and have a different audience in mind. If my parents were here, they would quietly question my good sense in putting my head above the parapet like this.

My experience has been thankfully very different. I told them – but as a wry joke – of my first formal meal as a Fellow of King's College, Cambridge, my first faculty-level position. I had been invited with my wife to a welcome lunch (it did not occur to them that my wife as a young practising lawyer might not have the time for a lengthy lunch midweek). The fellow next to me, a very grand elderly man, who Owned Art and an Estate in France (as I learned), turned to me and said, 'Goldhill. That's a Jewish name, isn't it?' 'It is,' I replied. 'Tell me,' he asked, 'Where did you learn English?' I could joke about it, but did not forget it, as I have everything else about the lunch. King's College is one of the most liberal of all colleges, with a history of active celebration of its large gay community since the nineteenth century, and a tradition of left-wing activism. The insulting snobbery of that first lunch has not been repeated, and I am extremely fond of the place, where I have worked ever since. Yet, when I quietly pointed out to the Senior Tutor one year that the welcome dinner for the first-year students had been regrettably scheduled for Yom Kippur, a Jewish day of fasting and the most observed holy day in the religious calendar, I was told that the date for the dinner had been set three years earlier. I did point out that the date for Yom Kippur had been set more than five thousand years before the catering committee's decision.

Wry jokes, then. No fuss. Even with the rise in tensions within the university around Middle Eastern politics, apart from the occasional need to educate more blatant ignorance – the width of Israel from Jerusalem to Tel Aviv it is not 300 miles but 30 – the norm in my experience is respectful if not always comprehending interaction. I worked for four years for UNESCO in Jerusalem with Israelis, Jordanians and Palestinians, primarily city planners and environmental activists, on a project about shared heritage;[17] subsequently, I ran a four-year international project in Cambridge for people who worked on or in the Middle East who could not normally or formally meet, to discuss city planning, water management and citizenship in the region – four years of intense and often painfully difficult, private group

---

[17]'The Programme for Understanding Shared Heritage' (PUSH), funded by the EU and the Norwegian Government, with UNESCO support.

discussions, but, granted the issues and the stakes, these debates were remarkably civil and punctuated with more laughter and sadness than hate.[18] I have been lucky enough to have the opportunity to carve out an intellectual space of activism, with groups of policy-makers, activists and academics, in the hope of making some small directed difference amid the rising aggression, anger and turn to violence in and beyond the region – and the continuing rise of express anti-Semitism in international and local politics in many places in the world, a particularly grim background against which to strive to make research instrumental or salient.

The debate over Christian anti-Jewish writing flares repeatedly into virulence in scholarship on late antiquity: there's a constant battle over the polemics, made especially painful by the religious authorization of later murderous violence, like the Crusades and pogroms, as much as by the Church's involvement in the Shoah. The Gospels ground this rhetoric: Matthew, alone of the Gospels (27.25), has the crowd respond to Pilate with, 'His blood be on us *and our children*,' a line quoted and requoted to justify violence against later generations of Jews, as if self-willed (the victims here literally 'ask for it');[19] and John's Gospel also influentially excoriates the Jews as a collective, rather than specifying a section of the Jewish people or its leaders.[20] But it is how the Fathers took on the Gospels in their rhetoric that moulds the tradition of Christianity's anti-Judaism. John Chrysostom's eight homilies against

---

[18]'The Topography of Citizenship', in my capacity as John Harvard Professor of Social Sciences and Humanities at Cambridge: thanks to the John Harvard Chair electors for this opportunity. One product is Goldhill, ed. (2020).

[19]See, saliently, John Chrysostom *Adv. Iud.* 6.1.1.

[20]John uses the words 'the Jews' 71 times; the synoptic gospels together 16 times. Azar (2016) is painfully apologetic. Reinhartz (2005) describes how her personally strained scholarly attempt to befriend the Beloved Disciple led her, a Jewish feminist mother, to be misidentified as a Catholic nun by her class; Reinhartz (2018) continues and closes her jagged distaste for this impossible friendship. Perry (2021) notes evangelical embarrassment at translating 'the Jews' in the new English Standard Version.

the Jews are paradigmatic. The first programmatic sermon can show what I mean. John Chrysostom is writing in Antioch in the fourth century, and his aim is to stop any of his congregation going to synagogue or participating in Jewish festivals.[21] He demands a radical separation between Christians and Jews: 'Why are you mixing what cannot be mixed?' (4.3.6). To make his case for purity, he launches a string of attacks on Jews that anticipate a familiar set of strategies of later racist rhetoric.

So, John repeatedly calls the Jews 'animals', and specifically 'dogs', an insult with a long afterlife.[22] When I was writing my book about Jerusalem, I spent a good deal of time sitting and talking with old men in cafés: one told me how when he was in the Turkish Army, when he was asked his name by an officer, he was required to reply, because he was Jewish, 'I am a dog and the son of a dog.'[23] Jews, for John, have a *sungeneia* (2.1) with dogs, a 'shared kinship'. But the generic language of animals (*probata, alogoi, thêria*) is even more common in John's attacks, and for a reason. As fattened animals, says John, Jews are no good for work, but they are 'fit for killing' [*sphagê*] (2.6). Turning the other cheek? 'This is why Jesus said . . . Bring them here and slay them.' Once the other is bestialized, slaughter is not far off.

The Jews reject the rule of Jesus (and John). How dare the Jews not realize, he expostulates (5.4), that the Books of Moses are really prophecies of Jesus (which is why the use of the 'Old Testament' is so offensive as an appropriative term: it assumes the self-evidence and truth of Christian typology with its violent history)? The cause of Jewish 'stubbornness', John declares, is 'gluttony and drunkenness' (2.5).[24] As ever, the despised other must be corrupt in bodily form, and

[21]On Antioch, see Sandwell (2011), with Eshelman (2012).
[22]Stow (2006).
[23]Goldhill (2008).
[24]See de Wet (2019).

must pervert privileged sociality. So, Jews dance 'like drunkards' in the street (2.7). The synagogue is full of 'faggots' (*malakoi,* a designedly nasty word) and 'whores' (2.7): it is a 'brothel, a theatre, a brigands' cave, a lair of wild-beasts' (3.1).[25] Sexuality, of course, is a telling part of this denigration: Jews are 'sex-mad like stallions' (6.8). The Jews are violent: they strike their fellow men (2.6) (John's aggression is thus pre-emptively prompted by the projected aggression of the other: Jews 'trample', 'break', 'destroy' the laws). Jews are 'stiff-necked' – as if the only reason for not being Christian is misunderstanding or resistance to truth. Jews are 'miserable and pitiable' (the starting point of the sermon [1.5/2.1]) but they are also 'frightening' (3.7). The contradictions – miserable yet frightening, effeminate but hypersexual, louche but violent – again are familiar from modern racist discourse. But John ups even this rhetoric. Jews, he declares, do not simply have 'demons in their souls' (6.6), they *are* 'demons' (*daimones* 6.3) – literally 'demonized'. They exhibit a transcendent 'blood guiltiness' (*miaiphonia*) because they 'sacrifice their own sons and daughters to demons' (6.7), a wild and bizarre climax of insult. They are thus 'even more savage than wild beasts' (6.7).

John promises that his tirade is offered as a cure for the sickness of wanting to mix with Jews – this language of sickness is pervasive and moralized, as is the rejection of any suggestion of hybridity. So, too, is the promise of punishment if you do not take the cure. The naturalness of health is made to support and veil the self-interest of the tirade, which defines its own perspective as the normal and necessary: the 'healthy'.[26] There is also an agenda here. As becomes clear (7.7–11), his congregants have been going to synagogues to get medical help. This practice, John declares, utilizing the language of the Gospels, is

---

[25]Sensible discussion in Drake (2013: 78–98).
[26]See Cook (2019) and Mayer (2015a and 2015b).

tantamount to saving the body but losing your immortal soul. His rhetoric also inevitably turns to military order. If a soldier abroad found a traitor in the army's midst, he would tell the general for the safety of them all. You must be an army for Christ, declares John (4.9).[27] There must be a war against the threat of the Jews, the cause of disease.

John knows all this from personal experience. Racist discourse always needs its personal witness, the man who knows and puts himself on the line. So, John tells how he himself saw a 'free woman, good-looking, modest, a Christian believer' dragged into a synagogue (our women are in danger!) and forced to take an oath (3.4). John describes how he upbraided the 'brutal unfeeling man' who committed this outrage, and brought him back into the fold. 'I will risk my life,' he asserts, 'rather than neglect anyone who is sick like this' (4.8). The demand for complicity, made in the passionately asserted personal truth of the speaker, is marked. He knows; he was there.

John felt the need to deliver eight such sermons, over the short period of the main Jewish holidays,[28] sermons so long and virulent that he went hoarse (he tells us, 6.1.3) but carried on, to make sure that the other is firmly separated and despised as other: John is instrumental in creating an image of 'the Jews', which has continued to be echoed down the centuries. Doesn't John's rhetoric look like textbook racism? Not just insulting a group as a group but turning them into animals, demonizing them, sexualizing them, medicalizing them as unhealthy causes of disease, manipulating the contradictions of fear and denigration, the threat to purity, to 'our women', proclaiming the need for war, leading to the normalization of violence. Sound

---

[27]See 3.1.2, 4.1.4, 4.3.4 and 6.1.
[28]Generally agreed that the first two were delivered in 386, the last six in 387.

disgustingly familiar? These homilies duly appear on today's anti-Semitic websites.[29]

I can do the formal analysis of this rhetoric, and, well trained, I did try to describe it without the evaluative adjectives that kept crowding in on my prose: but who would *not* want to say no to such nastiness, to judge it?[30] It may be painful but it is both necessary and insightful to read this text ethically, to see why his desire to make his community pure is also the 'teaching of contempt'.[31] Yet, the really vexing question is why, then, has this collection of sermons and other such speeches been systematically excluded from the current, heated discussions of whether there is racism or proto-racism in antiquity? It doesn't matter if you go to Ben Isaac's seminal book, which has forty pages on 'ancient attitudes to Jews', or to more recent discussions, such as Denise McCoskey's, which rightly stress the institutional racism of classics and its systematic whitening of the field, there is no significant discussion of this foundational Christian rhetoric.[32] As if Christians in antiquity were not also Greeks and Romans.[33] As if this rhetoric did not have an extended and horrific heritage. As if 'the teaching of contempt' has no impact. These long and interwoven histories of the rhetoric of violent self-aggrandizement have worked out so that I do not currently face the jagged teeth of this prejudice in my professional or personal life, as others certainly do today, day by day. But ignoring the strategies and instrumentality of writing like John's homilies only serves to oversimplify not just the past but also the internal dynamics

---

[29]References in Mayer (2019).

[30]The question is rhetorical, but a response might start from Nelson (2017), a study of unsentimental women, though not without the historical background in Chandler (2013) and Dixon (2017).

[31]Stroumsa (1996: 7), following the work of Jules Isaac.

[32]McCoskey (2012) and MacSweeney et al. (2019); Padilla Peralta (2021).

[33]Gager (1983) includes pagan and Christian material. Schäfer (2009), and e.g. Kennedy, Roy and Goldman (2013), however, are more typical in excluding any Christian material.

of the discipline, which continues to fail to recognize the complexity of its own complicities with institutional power and, for that matter, with revolution. This silence places me – us – on a map which I do not wish to inhabit.

In this case, indeed, there is an insidious, shared professional injunction that helps explain why these texts have been sidelined. If you are a classicist or a historian, you are likely to have responded to the previous paragraphs by insisting that we cannot judge ancient rhetoric by modern standards and we have to historicize it. After all, we know that the language of modern biological and national 'race' and 'racism' are not matched in antiquity (and John does not use *genos* or *ethnos* to refer to the Jews). Different styles of language matter. I agree. Always historicize, as Frederic Jameson sloganized.[34] But that does not mean historicize *away*. It means understand the consequences and responsibility of your own and others' positioning in time. When John is discussed, especially in theological writing, the Jews tend to disappear in a welter of apology that explains that John is really concerned with Christians, Christians who Judaize. So, one standard modern treatment of John Chrysostom's eight speeches insists that John's anti-Judaic rhetoric emerges from intra-Church concerns, and is 'more than a masterly example of pulpit invective' (to take an admiring reader's summary).[35] This understanding is generally agreed. Even David Nirenberg writes, 'Of course, John's rivals, Christian or pagan, were not really Jews, any more than the Jews were John's real rivals.'[36] John Chrysostom, Cyril of Alexandra and Origen,

---

[34]Jameson (1981): its first words (ix).

[35]The very influential Wilkens (1983); quotation from Kelly (1985: 483). The bibliography on the *adversus Iuadaeos* tradition, and John Chrysostom's place in it, is huge: see, most recently, the massive de Wet and Mayer (2019) and especially Mayer (2019) for references and discussion.

according to such an argument, 'reveal remarkably similar approaches to John's Gospel and its "Jews", that stem not from hostility towards contemporary Jews, but from both the allegorical mode of reading in which they were trained and their paraenetic concern for their own ecclesial communities'.[37] For this critic, it seems, the Gospel of John writes only about 'Jews', not Jews, and the later Fathers write *allegorically* about these 'Jews', a Platonic third remove from a 'real Jew' (as Annie Hall's grammy would call Woody Allen). A '"Jew"', then, or perhaps a '""Jew"""'. Really. Actually, really, it was the Jews, not '"the Jews"', that Cyril of Alexandria, one of the episcopal 'impressarios of urban violence',[38] expelled from the city in 414.

It is very strange to be interpellated like this, from antiquity and from today. When do the wry jokes stop? The personal voice becomes more insistent the more it is unrecognized or silenced.

And – you will know this – it's amazing how easy it is to tell me not to take it personally. No fuss. And, yes, it makes me uncomfortable to have brought it up at all. Easier to pass it by in silence, to pass, as my parents advised. Or maybe raise a polite and quizzical scholarly eyebrow. Yet, the long history of stereotypical abuse continues to have a powerful instrumental effect in contemporary politics, for so many individuals who find themselves caught up in this sort of 'allegory', this self-righteous and destructive 'paraenetic concern' (the vocabulary is part of the distancing, as if being concerned for your community justifies vitriolic attacks on others), this set of inverted commas that force the individual into a collective to be mistreated. As others know better than me, it doesn't take much

---

[36]Nirenberg (2013: 115).

[37]Azar (2016: 7).

[38]Frederiksen and Ishai (2006: 1004) – of bishops from the end of the fourth century, onwards.

to turn the distancing of inverted commas into the cruelty of shackles. So, yes, this time, it's personal.

iv Label me

The British public, I have been told since I was old enough to understand the sentences, would not put up with being required to carry an identity card, as many do in European countries. The suspicion of state control over such information or the policing that might follow from such a system, has made the imposition of such a requirement a political impossibility. 'Imagine, then,' said a security maven – a fellow whose shady job made him more at home in a le Carré novel than in the academic seminar on security I was chairing at the British Academy – 'Imagine if we had suggested that everyone should carry an electronic device that would allow us to track their movements in real time, get their personal history, and listen in to their private conversations. Political meltdown! Yet that is exactly what mobile phones have done; and people pay handsomely for the privilege.' There is a great deal of confusion about what personal information is – how it can or should be voiced – and how worried anyone should be about the dissemination of the personal. As a public health official reflected: 'Most people would have no anxiety about their post-code [zip code] being made public; but would be very cautious about their genetic code being open to all. But in the vast majority of cases the post-code is a much more accurate predictor of your long-term health prospects.'

On a card or elsewhere, identity is beginning to garner a rather bad name as a way of talking about people, after a decent run at opening up a political space of discussion. Identity is now being queried as part of the political trivialization of issues of diversity, hierarchy and power.[39] It has been absolutely crucial in specific situations to be able to say, 'As a ... I find that unacceptable/misguided/untruthful': this is the rhetoric of personal authority. Such labels have been empowering and instrumental in resisting the imposition of oppressive and uncontested norms. Yet – and this is where the bad name (and Shteyngart's comedy) starts from – such single titles have the potential to flatten multiple trajectories, desires and positions into a single, simple stereotype: as often as not, the projection of exactly the sort of categorization being resisted. Such (self-)labelling, however politically expedient, however convenient a gesture, is also always complicit with the oversimplification of the narratives of the self, which is the very structure of prejudice, racism, the blinkers of unawareness. This pushback is paradigmatic in feminist circles, where the very category of woman has been challenged by the addition of qualifiers from race, class, sexuality, financial security, age, circumstance with increasing nuance and purchase.[40] Not only are multiple identities embodied in any one person, as Kwame Anthony Appiah has eloquently argued, but such identities are also fissured by contingency; they shift in and over time, and are precariously inhabited, temporary closure misrecognized as stability.

Many surveys these days proudly declare that you can self-determine the categories of your identity. The well-publicized cases of two women who declared themselves Black, and tried to live within and benefit from such an identity, when there was no genealogy to support their claims, may be painful, but they also emphasize that it is

[39]Particularly influential have been Appiah (2005, 2006, 2014) and, in terms of gender, Butler (1999).
[40]A long and rich history, in which hooks (1981) and Collins ([1990] 2000) are especially influential, and, from another angle, Butler (1999) and Moi (1999); see also Collins (2019), which can stand for the potentially vast bibliography on the much used and, it seems, feared term, 'intersectionality'.

very risky, indeed, to think that identity can be simply and solely self-determined.[41] Identity is formed in dynamic social exchanges, where others' reactions also inform not only self-understanding but also the performance of the self: support and care, like violence and hate, transform identity. Identity is shaped in and by performance. ('If I am not what you say I am, you are not who you say you are.') It is both this necessary dynamic and the uncertainty of self-knowledge (as both Freud and Greek tragedy insist) that make it necessary to be very cautious about proclaiming the truth of the stories you tell about yourself. When a man tells women he is not sexist, his announcement may receive an eye-roll rather than an affirmation: the judgement cannot be solely up to him. (It is thus all the more surprising – indeed, ludicrous and insulting – that so many modern politicians and scholars seem to think that they themselves are the best judges of whether they themselves are anti-Semitic or racist.) How you tell your own story opens a minefield of retrospective justification, failed memories, heroic fantasies and slow understanding, as well as the lure of cliché, narrative form and sheer hopefulness. Such stories are also always told from somewhere and in a specific situation: an exchange, designed to do something. It's always crucial to work out what a story is *doing*. The labels of identity can help the story along – we need our stereotypes, shortcuts and icons. But recognizing the insufficiency of such labels is also an ethical injunction. Perhaps the greatest intellectual achievement in Karl-Ove Knausgaard's *My Struggle*, to my mind the most remarkable, excoriating literature of self-exposure, is the 400-page excursus on what it might mean to call Hitler evil,

---

[41]Rachel Dolezal and Jessica Krug. Rachel Dolezal was sacked from the Africana Studies programme at Eastern Washington University when it was revealed that she had two white parents: she claimed to self-identify as Black; Jessica Krug resigned from George Washington University when it was revealed that her racial self-identification was not based on her parentage.

complete with readings of Celan's poetry – not to challenge that Hitler was an evil man, but to understand the when, why, what and where of this horrific person, from his own self-representation and from others' attempts to fathom how he became evil.[42]

Sexual identity, where 'orientation' or 'preference' has become integral to modern thinking, is an exemplary discourse where the other is deemed crucial to self-definition. Here, labelling is paradigmatically reduced to letters: LGBQT (and so on). In the face of legal and often violent social denigration, and the corresponding political movements that have not yet finished changing society, it has become taken for granted that sexual orientation/preference means that the person you desire sexually defines who you are in an integral or even essential way. That is, the object of your desire by virtue of its objectification defines the self. For the most traditional normative thinking , this has led to the paradoxical and unacceptable ethical conclusion that the man who has violent abusive sex with a woman is normatively preferable to the man who has gentle, caring sex with a man. For whom can that be right?

Here is a place where the study of ancient sexuality may help us think about modernity and its contingencies more clearly and reflectively. We can start with dreams, the royal road, as Freud put it. Artemidorus is the first theorist we know to have written a book about dream analysis. His *Traumdeutung* makes for fascinating reading. When a man reports a dream that he has had sex with his mother, the first follow-up question Artemidorus suggests a doctor should ask is, 'In what position?' I am not sure that would be the first thought of most psychoanalysts today. For Artemidorus, *how* you have sex with your mother is much more interesting analytically than the fact that it is your mother. For Artemidorus, the mother will

---

[42]Knausgaard (2012–18), vol. 6, aptly titled, *The End: My Struggle*.

naturally indicate the motherland, so how you have sex with her will express a profound sense of your political relation to the country or city where you were born. This is not a perverse thought, in antiquity at least. On the one hand, the expectation that one's public political life is crucial, even dominant, in self-definition is a reliable annoyance to bourgeois self-obsession with privacy and inwardness – a dark mirror from the past. On the other hand – and this is the crucial lesson – it has become a commonplace of our contemporary debates about ancient sexuality that object-oriented concepts of desire, which so dominate modern thinking, find a striking contrast in antiquity which do not tend to organize thinking about sexual preference around objects so much as processes. What would the world look like if we did learn from antiquity? If the answer to the question about sexual orientation was not a gender or an object but a process or a relation? Imagine the world where you might say my sexual orientation is towards gentleness. My preference is towards self-delusion followed by hysterical recrimination. My orientation is towards over-idealized cathexis leading to inevitable disappointment. My preference is emotional disconnect combined with aggression, narcissism to the point of manipulating desire into callousness ... What is more significant, more definitional as a mark of identity, *who* you desire or *how* you desire? Which is more *personal*?

The stories we tell of ourselves come at a cost, and always say both more and less than we desire or know. We might hope that locating the personal voice and mobilizing it should lead to self-awareness above self-display – an awareness of the veils, lures and misprisions of self-representation, the inadequacies as well as the demands of self-knowledge. As the *Odyssey* constantly reminds us, to identify yourself is also to be recognized – which is to open the scars of the past and to perform the narrative of the self again. It *should* be difficult to tell the story of the 'I'. I wonder whether classics, with its sense of historical contingency and change, could not lead a more robust evaluation of the cost of the current, strident strategies of self-labelling?

v A sentimental education

For generations in the West, reading the texts of classical antiquity has been made integral to *Bildung*, the formative accession to culture. (And, for sure, such accession is matched by exclusion, too.) But this exemplarity is always fissured by loss and distance, the inability of the present to match the exemplarity of the past, fully and adequately. To see a statue of the bare-chested George Washington in a toga is to visualize the aspiration and the impossibility of classical exemplarity.

To tell your own story is to make an example of yourself. A story told from a point in time, which remoulds the past from a present perspective. The conversion narrative is the archetype of such stories, where the past becomes significant as the prelude to the moment – or process – of change, which can only be perceived from the now of the achieved transformation.[43] As classical antiquity has been repeatedly used to reform the present, both in revolution and in conservative resistance to change, so we use the stories of our education as classicists to explain how we have become who we are. Our personal voice rings with a sentimental education.

The figure of the schoolmaster is a vivid figure of the imaginary, from childhood on: Dr Arnold – at one level – in *Tom Brown's Schooldays*, an icon for the development of muscular Christianity as an educational ideal; at another level, the schoolmaster, Kulygin, in Chekhov's *Three Sisters*, giggling at his wife's lover for his childhood inability to master *ut* and the subjunctive; at another level still, the roll

---

[43]Goldhill (2020: 149–93) for discussion and bibliography.

call of teachers in Harry Potter's Hogwarts, with their Latin-sounding spells. As academics, we tell our stories to ourselves and others through our icons of teaching and research. There is always someone we cannot live up to, some model earnestly to deny. In making an example of ourselves, we have our examples in mind.

My personal voice as an academic is layered between my past and the past: how I encountered and continue to encounter antiquity and my own memories. I have been reading Homer and Greek tragedy for nearly fifty years now (in those days, it all started in the classroom at school aged nine, not, as for Jack Winkler, with great stories and great bodies, but with grammar, vocabulary lists and stories that were far beyond my ken).[44] It is beyond me – though I know examples – how anyone can read tragedy for so long and still simply take at face value the stories we tell each other about ourselves. It seems such a failure of the lauded *Bildung* of a classical education. What I loved about Daniel Mendelsohn's, *An Odyssey: A Father, a Son, an Epic* (2017) – it made me envious, actually, to mark the affect more truly – were the elegant juxtapositions and intertwining of his classroom experience as a teacher, his family relationship with his father and his reading of the *Odyssey*, with its hero of deception and the manipulation of self-representation. (Could a woman, Helen Morales asks me, tell the same sort of story? I am not sure. It's complicated. Perhaps Emily Wilson will write about how her father, the polemical and error-prone writer A. N. Wilson, haunts her translation, her career. I'd want to read that. But she would be hard pressed to find a satisfactory *ancient* text to base her story on.) More even than in *The Elusive Embrace*, Mendelsohn's first memoir, or in *The Lost*, his family history, this, his third personal exploration, insists that work is personal and the personal is hard work.[45]

---

[44]I am referring to the autobiographical opening of Winkler (1990).
[45]Mendelsohn (1999, 2006 and 2017).

Mendelsohn's name starts *men de* (as he joked many years ago): on the one hand (*men*), he has the confidence to express his doubts and insufficiencies as a son, a teacher, a person; on the other (*de*), he lets the figure of Odysseus, the tricky bastard, stand at the centre of his self-representation, a different mask, a man who lies to his father. It's a very smart performance. But what needs emphasizing is how integrated the personal and the professional are in his story. This speaks to me. My voice, my perspective, my self-understanding – how I inhabit the world – have been significantly formed by my reading and teaching: my continuing education. The search for the affective and personal in the work of criticism is mirrored by the recognition of the work of criticism in the affective and personal. My education – which is, of course, more than my degrees or work in an educational institution – is not an added skill, like riding a bicycle, but integral to *who I am*. My feelings – my personal voice, how I see the world – are *educated*: a sentimental education.

There are many reasons why Augustine's *Confessions* moves me and has become a compulsive return in my current thinking (for all that I read as a resistant, stubborn, Jew, objectified by his writing). Of course, the text is brilliant and serious in its desperate articulation of the travails of self-exploration, and stunningly articulate in its analysis of how time and memory play a role in understanding the self and the stories the self tells. It is anguished in its recognition of the failures and deceptions of the self. But I am also transfixed that after the remarkable narrative of how he came to convert to Orthodox Christianity, and after the extraordinary theoretical exegesis of memory and time – a moment when many readers of Augustine stop – he proceeds to give an analytic account of interpretations of Genesis: a solid theological exegesis. Genesis – the account of creation – has been fundamental to the whole of the *Confessions*, as has his own wonder at where he himself comes from (in all senses). But what these final books insist upon is that the Christian is made by and exists in a relationship to texts and reading – an engagement with the *logos*. For Augustine, how the Bible is to be read is an absolutely integral part of what it is to be. There is more, for sure: grace, God's will, that which transcends the self. But as any self-respecting feminist or queer theorist or political scientist also knows, there is no issue of separating theory from experience, only a question of how to negotiate their inevitable intertwining in a life, in how you inhabit the world and speak out.

Perhaps the most compelling question asked by the theoretical turn to the personal voice is to imagine the psychology that still insists on no more than an impersonal voice.

vi Self-explanation

A few years ago, I wrote a book called *A Very Queer Family Indeed*. It was based on a great deal of archival research – I am still, I think, the only person alive to have read all 180 volumes of Arthur Benson's diary (Henry James read a few volumes with polite interest).[46] The Bensons were a family of graphomaniacs, who between them published not only over a 100 volumes of novels and essays, but also autobiographies and biographies of each other, which, along with their extant letters, and their extensive footprint in the public life of Victorian and Edwardian Britain – Arthur's father, Edward White Benson, was Queen Victoria's Archbishop of Canterbury – allowed for a uniquely rich understanding of the internal dynamics of a uniquely surprising family. The book was not the biography of a family but an analysis of three crucial elements of how this family tellingly

---

[46]Goldhill (2016b).

uncovered the social tensions and transitions between the Victorian and Edwardian eras in Britain. First, it looked at the remarkable map of sexuality that they inhabited/inhibited, across a period when the pathology and vocabulary of 'homosexuality' was being invented (none of the six children of the archbishop ever had heterosexual intercourse; his wife spent her last twenty years sharing a bed with the daughter of the previous Archbishop of Canterbury, in a house with her daughter, who was also sharing a bed with her own female companion); second, it explored the role of religion in this family – how the children responded to their father's intense crusading faith, and their mother's personal spiritual sense; third, it considered the role of life-writing – how producing stories about themselves and their friends and heroes was integral to their life: this was a family which wrote itself. It was a book in which tracing the personal voice through paraded reticence and selective frankness was an obsessive activity for me.

In explaining why I was not writing a family biography, but about the historical developments of biographical writing, sexual self-representation and religion, through one family's interactions, I cited the bravado observation of the psychoanalyst and literary critic Adam Phillips that biography is a ludicrous genre. This was said, knowingly, in his brilliant biography of Freud.[47] I thought that by noting that the phrase 'ludicrous genre' actually sprang from a sophisticated and admired example of the genre, it would be enough to warn readers of a certain irony at work. (I should have known better.) Biography is a ludicrous genre, for a psychoanalyst at least, because of its pretensions of understanding, comprehensiveness and narrative clarity. Writing stories about lives is basic to Freudian case histories, as exploring reasons for a person's (in)decisions, analysing the psychopathology of

---

[47]Phillips (2014).

everyday life, and tracing the compulsions and confusions of lived experience, are fully part of psychoanalysis as a discipline. What seemed ludicrous to Adam Phillips – and, for that matter, to me – is the idea of summarizing a messy life in a few hundred pages of chronological narrative, as if the intricate, fragmented internal life of a person, the most intimate personal sense of self, could be plumbed by another, thus. I was always conscious as I read through the millions of words of Arthur Benson's diary that he began it by stating bluntly, 'There are two things I will never say' in the diary – and these two most personal, shrouded secrets remain secrets.

Yet, a couple of critics got very hot under the collar that I appeared to be dismissive of biography as a genre, and declared I should have written a jolly biographical account anyway. So, with that in mind, I want here to try to be as explicit and direct as I can be about why I have written as I have about the personal voice in scholarship, without a personal biography. I have not offered a list of nouns and adjectives to describe myself – criticism is not an episode of *Blind Date* or *The Bachelor* – nor have I tried to express how my background, with a few self-defensive sentences about the complexities of privilege, has affected my criticism; familiar strategies, both. Everyone, of course, is a figure of their time and place and everyone has a personal story, but *how* you are formed by your own situatedness is neither a simple determinism, nor simply available to self-knowledge. I have offered fragments of a personal voice about the personal voice because these narratives of the self cannot be complete or whole: just case histories. I want to resist what I see as naïve identity politics, embodied in paraded and demanded labels. By which I mean: it is one thing to recognize the rallying power of the label, the slogan, the stereotype. Sometimes the blank assertion of 'I am,' like a good scream or an explosive curse word, feels like the only adequate response. But the instrumental power of such labels for destructiveness, divisiveness and oppression cannot be forgotten. Emotion, like the narratives of identity, also requires political nuance if it is to be mobilized responsibly and instructively. I'd like to think that criticism – what we *do* – has a more transformative and significant political role to play in articulating and promoting how the complexity of cultural interactions and productions can be understood. Not by denying the personal voice, but by articulating it with attention, purposiveness, and understanding: the responsibility of response. Hence, what I admire in Catherine Conybeare's recent article on the *Liber Manualis* of the ninth-century Carolingian noblewoman Dhuoda, is her exemplary ability to recognize why and how and when the impersonal voice is a form of blindness and self-denial, rather than a commitment to objective scholarship – and her skill in showing how such impersonal rhetoric has distorted the modern critical account of the family history she is analysing – without trivializing or oversimplifying the place from where she herself is speaking. One could even imagine a manifesto: to see the personal voice not as the denied other of ideal scholarly practice, but as an integral, intricate, *intimate* vector within it.

What I should have said in Seattle, then, was something like this. You have asked me to talk about my personal investment in classical scholarship and the discipline in which I have spent my working life. What is this personal voice? The first thing to emphasize is that to talk of the self is a far from trivial matter: it is extremely difficult to understand yourself, or, for that matter, to narrate your self adequately. Often, the hardest question to answer properly, knowingly is, 'What do you want?' So, my immediate reaction is caution, but also excitement at such a good question.

But that is certainly not enough, nor an answer. I do think that the situatedness of a scholar – where you speak from – is integral not just to the scholarly voice but also to the possibility of responsibility in scholarship. And responsibility should not be an optional extra to scholarship, but a requirement of it. So, let me try three things I dislike in the current debates about situatedness and the personal voice. The first concerns religion: it is fascinating that for all the confessional modes in classical criticism – gender, sexuality, race are all upfront in such culture wars – religion is largely taboo. So, when I read the texts of late antiquity with their virulent anti-Jewish rhetoric, and when I read scholars who comment on such language, I am not expected to take it personally. I am certainly not expected to talk about it publicly. I dislike my confusion of feeling that results: on the one hand, my anger at the viciousness of such language, its continuing political purchase and my annoyance when scholars explain away its virulence or impact; and, on the other hand, my socially trained embarrassment at mentioning such a personal matter. Drawing attention to the difference to me. What I dislike, that is, is what the tradition of such discourse – the thoughtless exercise of Christian norms and expectations – does to me.

The second thing I dislike follows immediately from what I have just said. I fully accept the instrumental power of declaring who you are with a simple and single statement of identity. There are times when it does feel that the only thing to shout out is, 'I am a . . .', 'I speak as a . . .' I just now nearly wrote, 'does to me, *as a Jew*'. But I heard the inspirational James Baldwin in my head (with the immediate and necessary recognition that my case was not his): 'I am not your Jew.' Such slogans can motivate, bond, criticize and empower. But I immediately also want to qualify, nuance, narrate. To recognize that stereotyping and prejudice depend on denying the qualification, nuance and narration in the name of a slogan or label. The second thing I dislike is when such labels become the dominant means and matter of debate about who you are. Part of our responsibility is to recognize and respect the historical depth and complexity of our own and others' positionality. To take the time and care to treat the personal with that much attention.

The third dislike follows on, too. One good answer to the question, 'What do you teach?' is 'people'. There are, we know, some administrators and politicians who think education is no more than the transmission of facts or techniques from an expert to a student, a process which a computer could do pretty well. But critical reading, responsibility, ethical citizenship, understanding the world through more than its physical instantiations, requires a more complex sense of what is undertaken in a university – and in society. At the turning point of the invention of the modern university, this process of education was called *Bildung*: a personal transformation into culture. The integration of intellectual enquiry and the way a life is lived seems to me to be inevitable. How we think and are trained to think and reflect on our thinking is part of who we are and how we inhabit our world and contribute to society. So, the third thing I dislike is the assumption, embodied in an approach to the discipline, that the proper academic voice is designedly and necessarily impersonal.

So, *how* the personal voice is integrated into what we do remains an ongoing question for the discipline, not an answer, and my three dislikes are about significant ways in which the personal is oversimplified in current discourse. I don't know if that answers your question as you hoped (I would conclude to the graduate). I have offered fragments because answers to such hard questions must be partial, contingent, temporary (like identity itself). But let's continue to discuss. And I will have another glass of wine.[48]

---

[48]Many thanks to my dear friends, Helen Morales and Catherine Conybeare, who discussed this chapter with me at length.

2

What Is a Jewish Classicist?

For Miriam Leonard; a wonderful friend,
for twenty-five years (and counting).

i Doing religion

When I was about to become director of CRASSH, the Centre for Research in Arts, Social Sciences and Humanities, the interdisciplinary research centre of the University of Cambridge, I spoke with its outgoing director, Mary Jacobus, the distinguished psychoanalytic critic and Professor of English Literature, about my intention to apply for a €2.5 million European Research Council Advanced Grant with a project titled, 'The Bible and Antiquity in 19th-Century Culture'. This project aimed to explore how the Bible and classical antiquity provided different models of the past as genealogies of modernity, and to investigate how these different models interrelated in Victorian thinking. 'At CRASSH,' Mary replied simply, 'we don't do religion.' I explained that it was not an evangelical project (of course), but an intellectual, multidisciplinary history that would include the gurus of modernism, Nietzsche, Freud, Darwin, along with, say, William Marshall, one of the founders of modern economics, whose history of economics started in ancient Greece, or Richard Wagner whose revolutionary theories and practice of modern music explicitly were founded on an idealized Hellenic antiquity. 'We don't do religion,' repeated Mary, even more strongly.

It would take a great deal of work to outline here the multiple ways in which the modern university, by virtue of its secular principles, finds religion a deeply uncomfortable subject, not least as it reminds the institution of its own long religious history, now strenuously disavowed.[1] But Mary was not just rehearsing the contemporary academic marginalization of religion as a subject. What I also recognized – I knew it well enough – was her own proud background as a feminist, left-wing Jew. For her, to be secular was an article of faith. Rita Thalmann – one of the great pioneers of women's history whose autobiographically informed work on Nazi Germany constantly articulates the interactions of racism and sexism – puts is amusingly: 'It is a blessing for France that it is a secular [*laïque*] state' (she just refrains from adding, 'thank God' to the blessing …).[2] For her, monotheistic 'religious practice', though not the culture of Judaism, is 'a barrier to the emancipation of women'. For Mary Jacobus, it seemed, a deeply held commitment to secularism would be tainted by a commitment to studying the Bible, even the Bible in the nineteenth century. 'We don't *do* religion,' is a mantra.

The grant application was successful, the project was located in CRASSH and a team of twelve academics spent five happy years researching its central questions. This opening anecdote can stand as an epigraph to what follows, not just because what I am to discuss

---

[1]Conybeare and Goldhill, eds (2020).
[2]Weber, ed. (1996: 118).

necessarily embraces this fascinating history of how modernity has engaged with the traditions of both the Hebrew Bible and classical antiquity, together and severally – the inevitable background to any discussion of modern Jewish receptions of antiquity – but also because the story highlights the intensely difficult issue of personal politics, identity and religion, which this chapter broaches. It has become a commonplace that scholarship is (to be) situated, that despite the ideology of objectivity there is no 'view from nowhere', and that each scholar's situatedness is an integral and even determinative factor in the practice of scholarship.[3] How a scholar is 'of her time'; how scholarship is marked by the networks of personal and institutional history; how practices of exclusion and inclusion affect the practices and (self-)understanding of intellectual pursuit, are questions that locate our understanding of a scholar's engagement (as we started to explore in Chapter 1).[4] Within such a nexus of politicized criticism, it becomes pressing to ask what it might mean to identify oneself or to be identified as a Jewish classicist.

The question, 'What is a Jewish classicist?' can immediately be sharpened. It is not hard to compose a list of classicists who happen to be Jewish. Some, like Jacob Bernays, might 'do religion';[5] others, like Eduard Fraenkel, might intently avoid any practice or outward signs of religious affiliation ('all trace of such a faith was removed from his personality'[6]); others still, like Charles Brink, might have converted

---

[3]Seminal is Haraway (1988).

[4]See *The Postclassicisms Collective* (2019: 144–60).

[5]See Momigliano (1994a), Grafton (1998), Bollack (1998), Porter (2015) and, more generally, Dunkelgrun (2020).

[6]Williams (1970: 440), 'and it was one of the few subjects on which a note of bitterness – or, perhaps, it was really irony – could creep into his voice'. We will return to the word 'personality'. On Fraenkel, see Stray (2014), shortened in Stray (2015). Williams' students have insisted to me about his deep decency as a mentor.

(twice, *noch*) to Protestant Christianity.[7] What is at stake thus is twofold. On the one hand, what does it mean to identify oneself or to be identified as Jewish? What sort of identification or affiliation – national, cultural, religious, personal or none of these –is being claimed or attributed? On the other hand, how does such an identification relate to the situatedness of a scholar? How are scholarship and Jewishness to be related? We could put the question like this. A woman who is a feminist classicist could properly and proudly say that both the subjects she chooses to work on and the way she works on them are integrally related to herself as a woman and a feminist; a Marxist similarly could insist that topics and methods are determined by her Marxist positionality. A Black classicist these days (and we will return to the generational aspects of these questions) is likely to claim that her work is informed not just by the toxic racism of society but also by the insidious prejudicial institutional forces within academia:[8] the past is studied from a position in the here and now of contemporary society, and comprehension of what the classical tradition is and means, will necessarily be framed by a sense of inclusion or exclusion. You are born female or Black; you choose to be a feminist or a Marxist; you can activate or repress your self-affirmation as a woman or a person of colour. But, in each case, how you identify yourself is seen to be integral to your work as a scholar. What, then, of being a Jewish classicist? To whom and when does the title 'Jewish scholar' make sense to affirm or deny? What lineaments of identification are brought

---

[7]For what Jaeger determined were nationalist motivations: Jocelyn (1994: 323): Brink converted twice, first, in Germany to evangelical Lutheranism, then in England to Anglicanism. Fraenkel resigned from the British Academy because Brink was elected (Stray 2014), though the reasons are unclear.

[8]Exemplary is Padilla Peralta (2021). Rankine (2006: 3–21, born in 1971), for example, is strikingly different in positionality from Frank Snowden (born 1911; Snowden 1970, 1983), let alone William Scarborough (born 1852), on whom see Ronnick (2000, 2011) and Ronnick, ed. (2005), Scarborough's extraordinary autobiography.

into play by such a title? This chapter will argue that these issues pose a set of searching questions for contemporary debates about situatedness, identity politics and disciplinary self-understanding, which are right at the centre of how the discipline of classics is currently interrogating its self-formation.

To research this complex and engaging question, I interviewed over thirty scholars who work on antiquity, each for an hour or more, about their sense of identification, affiliation and scholarly practice; I cross-referenced these with other scholars' perceptions. This set of semi-structured interviews (to use the technical description) has been combined with salient autobiographies of classical scholars, as well as obituaries, biographies, prefaces and methodological reflections of further scholars about their own and others' work. Also brought to bear are histories of classical scholarship and the voluminous literature on situatedness, identity politics and the institutional history of the discipline. Before I turn to some of the stories and provisional conclusions from this process, however, five general points need to be outlined.

First, the field of enquiry is inevitably shaped by the Second World War and the deep history of anti-Semitism (or, earlier, Judaeophobia), which culminated in the racist, genocidal violence of the Shoah.[9] Perhaps nobody simply became a classicist because of the Shoah, but so many life-stories of classicists were profoundly shaped by it. Pierre Vidal-Naquet witnessed his parents taken away to Auschwitz where they were murdered, and he himself survived only by the intervention of his teacher and friends who desperately warned him not to go home from school as usual.[10] Erich Gruen, at the last moment in 1939, managed to leave Vienna for the United States as a child with his

---

[9]See Nirenberg (2013), Stow (2006), Schäfer (2009) and Isaac (2004).
[10]Vidal-Naquet (1995: 55–160).

parents, fleeing because of anti-Jewish laws.[11] Jenny Strauss Clay was
born in Cairo during the war; her mother died in childbirth; she was
sent to a foster family in a kibbutz in Israel; her father, Eliezer Paul
Kraus, a brilliant Arabist, unemployed in Europe because of his
Jewishness, killed himself; and Jenny was sent from her foster family to
be brought up by her uncle in Chicago, Leo Strauss, whom she called
father.[12] The history of assimilation or assertion for Jews in Europe in
particular is haunted by the politics of the violent deixis that insists on
revealing Jews as religiously, physiologically, psychologically, morally,
politically corrupt or treacherous or, simply, other, and by the
consequent strategies of concealment and passing.[13] Jews have been
made visible, by yellow stars, the walls of the ghetto or by imaginary
physiognomics. (The impossibility of invisibility under the racism of
colour is most vividly and movingly articulated by Ralph Ellison's
Invisible Man.)[14] These specific historical dynamics of racism change
the politics of *naming*, of calling attention: of what Althusser would call
'interpellation' – of how one is called into culture.[15]

Second, the history of the university – and especially what we can
call the dominantly Protestant, but insistently secular universities of
the West – is intimately intertwined with the history of the liberal
nation state and its determination of the place of religion. As Cécile
Laborde has articulated most recently and sophisticatedly, partly in
response to the influential work of Charles Taylor, the liberal state
paradigmatically regards religion as a private matter (whether the
Church is disestablished or not).[16] Thereby, as Lena Salaymeh and

---

[11]For classics in the Third Reich, see the seminal Losemann (1977); also Losemann (2006),
Näf (1986) and Roche (2019).
[12]Kraemer (1999), Scrbacic (2013) and Strauss Clay (2003).
[13]Gilman (1985, 1991).
[14]On Ellison, see Rankine (2006).
[15]Althusser (1971).
[16]Laborde (2017), Taylor (2007); see also Asad (2003) and Mahmood (2015).

Shai Lavi remind us, both Islam and Judaism, because they insist on a public, political essence to practice, are misrecognized and marginalized.[17] This Protestant-coloured requirement that religion should be a matter of internal, private belief combines with the necessary secularism of modern academic disciplines to make a religious affiliation a mark of public embarrassment in a scholarly jurisdiction. To be marked as religious – 'weirdly exotic', as David Levene specified from New York, where exoticism is not necessarily sniffed at – is to be marked out as potentially making judgements based on faith not facts. At its most basic, as I stated in Chapter 1, any historical explanation that turns to Providence – God's hand – to explain causality, is properly rejected and thoroughly despised. That is simply not how modern history can or should be construed: indeed, modernity's Enlightenment principles can be defined as grounded in the denial of providential history. Differently from the battles which a feminist, Marxist or scholar of colour faces, religious confession in the secular university is likely therefore to appear, we have seen, as a perversity, an embarrassment. To announce a religious affiliation publicly is a risk for an academic's reputation. Why, then, wilfully search for an identification as a 'Jewish classicist'?

Third, because of the singular significance of the Shoah, generational and national differences have a special purchase. The proxemics of recognition for the Shoah have been subject to fascinating analysis. In the decades immediately after the war, the voice of the victims – the survivors primarily – was barely heard: Primo Levi's work became an iconic masterpiece only decades after it was first published (and, at first, systematically ignored).[18] Rather than teaching 'the Second

---

[17]Salaymeh and Lavi (2021).
[18]For the 'strongly enforced taboo on the public discussion of the Nazi era' in Germany until the 1960s, see Bialas and Rabinach, eds (2007: xvii), with extensive bibliography.

World War', a staple of curricula today, heads turned away, in a refusal to look hard at what was so painful and so painfully close. The children of both victims and perpetrators of horrific violence have been analysed, often through harrowing fiction as much as through psychoanalytic or historical exploration.[19] So, too, the politics of memory and memorial are bitterly contested. How distance from the Shoah is expressed or experienced affects what sort of affirmation of Jewishness is possible: my father's and my son's self-placement with regard to the Shoah, and thus to public self-recognition, cannot be the same as mine. So, the Harvard philosopher, Stanley Cavell, who changed his name from Goldstein to find out what it would be like 'if I did not simply announce my Jewishness by my name', struggles with his 'sense of [his] father's inner ghetto'.[20] Forms of distance, as Constanze Güthenke has discussed, are crucial to understanding academic engagement.[21]

At the same time, different national experiences distinctively influence a response to religious affiliation. This is not a matter of national stereotyping, but rather the specifics of a national history. A contrast between France and Britain is telling. Public discourse in France still reverts obsessively to the national scandal of the Dreyfus Affair, and the anguished recollections and denials of collaboration during the Second World War. The mass arrival of Sephardi Jews from the Maghreb and particularly from Algeria changed the demographics of the Jewish community in France and how it was perceived in wider society. Students in Paris in the 1960s could chant, 'We are German

---

[19]A huge bibliography on witnessing could be given, from the 1980s onwards especially (Bar-On 1989; and Felman and Laub 1992), though the works of Hannah Arendt remain seminal (1951, 1958, 1962). David Grossman's 1986 novel, *See Under: Love*, is hugely influential.
[20]Cavell (1994: 11, 24), during the Second World War.
[21]Güthenke (2020).

Jews,' a symbolic statement of support for the victims of prejudice and violence[22] – a protest unimaginable in Britain, where public discourse remains in systematic denial of its long and destructive involvement in the Middle East, even after the invasion of Iraq, and insists on a simple moral superiority of victory in the Second World War. There is no equivalent of the recognition of Algerian Jews alongside the Ashkenazi community. In French intellectual circles, Jewishness itself is a conceptual apparatus. Jean-François Lyotard can be asked, 'Would you say that all writers, according to your definition of writing, are Jews?' He replies: 'With inverted commas, yes, I would say so, but only with the reservation of inverted commas.'[23] This conversation – which will look all too French to Anglo-Saxon minds – is in a volume entitled, *Questions au Judaïsme*, involving seven distinguished French intellectuals in conversation about Jewishness – again, such a volume is hard to imagine in Britain – at least nowadays; at the time of Matthew Arnold, the opposition of Hellenism and Hebraism could be seen likewise as a matrix to comprehend and regulate culture, an opposition that runs through European intellectual history, as Miriam Leonard has superbly outlined, though Hebraism and Judaism certainly do not overlap in any straightforward manner.[24] The relationship of Derrida and Levinas, say, and specifically their mutually engaged constructions of the Jewishness of their thought, has been recognized as a crucial juncture in post-war French philosophy – a dialogue which has no equivalent in England.[25] In France, such an intellectual framework will inevitably change what the term 'Jewish classicist' can connote.[26] The contrast with Germany

---

[22]Fine analysis in Hammerschlag (2010).

[23]Weber, ed. (1996: 200).

[24]Leonard (2012), with further background in Leonard (2005). Shavit (1997), baggy and messy, looks from another angle.

[25]Hammerschlag (2016) is the fullest discussion of this.

[26]Simon-Nahum (2005).

is equally stark. Classics as a field 'has never really recovered' from the
damage of the Second World War, a German-trained philologist who
now works in England commented to me, but 'it is a completely
different experience reading *Antigone*' in Germany, because of the
different imbrications with – and education about – the Shoah, and
not just for the decades immediately after the war. Scholarship may be
international; but generational and national coordinates mark out the
contours of engagement with history, the horizons of expectation that
come from communal experiences. As we will see in Chapter 3, such
national coordinates are grounded in the strong sense of a specific
and much promoted ideal of German philology in the nineteenth
century – 'a peculiarly German science'[27] – adopted, admired, feared
and rejected by the rest of Europe and America. Such distances and
differences introduce a fragile core to what might be understood by
the title 'Jewish classicist'.

Fourth, contemporary politics also changes the contours of
identification. On the campuses of Western universities, there is likely
to be a good deal of heated and often ill-informed discussion of the
politics of the Middle East. To be Jewish is now inevitably not just to be
associated with Israel and the violent disagreements about its policies,
but also to be held publicly responsible. It is not an area where nuanced
positions about affiliation, belonging and political justice are rhetorically
easy to maintain. As one scholar who had left Britain to work in Israel,
reminisced knowingly with me: 'Why would I identify as a Jewish
scholar in Britain when all that would mean was "victim of anti-
Semitism"?' Her worry was not so much that she would be treated as an
heir to the Shoah's horror, but rather that the rhetoric of campus
hostilities would force her into positions of defence and accusation
because 'anti-Semitism' has become a token of insult and self-promotion

---

[27]Hart (1892: 280), quoted and discussed in the excellent Kurtz (2021).

rather than an analytic category of prejudice (not least because certain leading political figures, when it comes to anti-Semitism, have volubly demonstrated not just shocking levels of ignorance but also dim-witted self-justification of their ignorance). Public identification also involves the anticipation of response, an anticipation formed by the perception of the public understanding of such identification: social normativity functions by the projection of aggression towards the challenge of difference. For any minority, there is always a cost in asserting a politicized identity. In such an atmosphere, does it not seem sensible to hesitate before accepting the title 'Jewish classicist'?

Fifth, and finally, the disciplinary boundaries of classics with regard to theology are also a major factor in how antiquity is approached. Classics and theology have a long, intertwined history, much repressed in the current self-examination of classics as a discipline;[28] but one telling consequence of the separation of the fields in the modern academy is that the single most influential text of Hellenistic literature is systematically excluded from any classics course, and especially from courses on Hellenistic literature. The Septuagint is reserved for theologians, although the concept and practice of translation, cultural interaction between dominant and marginal groups, civic life and religion, and different levels of linguistic register (not to mention Jewish receptions of antiquity) are all topics of major research interest to classicists.[29] Similarly, as we have noted, the choice of Philo and Josephus as research topics for an academic career have historically proven to be gestures of self-marginalization, although the questions raised by such texts are central to the history of empire, the history of rebellion against empire and assimilation into it, the history from below of the subjects of empire and so on – that is, some of the most

---

[28]See Conybeare and Goldhill, eds (2020).
[29]Rajak (2009) is exceptional in this regard.

compelling of contemporary political and historical issues. So-called
early Christianity – that is, the texts of the Jewish writers who produced
the Gospels, Paul's letters and the early apologists – is rarely included
in the study of the early empire, although it is clearly the most
influential Greek prose of the period. (Jesus grew up under Augustus.)
Early Christianity is also an arena where religious affiliation is still an
aggressive badge of scholarly argument.[30] How *Jewish* Paul is, for
example, is a question likely to revert to how Jewish the scholars
discussing it are, in a way, as we will see, that would make mainstream
classicists squirm.[31] Adele Reinhartz tells the amusing counter-story
of how when she was teaching a course on the Gospel of John
(carefully), she – a Jewish, feminist, mother of four – was thought to
be a Catholic nun by an anxious Anglican student, worried about the
religious ideology of her teacher.[32] In the study of early Christianity, it
is taken for granted, it seems, that the religious identity of the scholar
is a salient factor: Reinhartz's book is structured precisely as the
encounter of a *Jewish* writer with the Gospel. The discomfort about
religious confession in classics is mirrored by its insistence within
theology – and enforced by the institutional separation of classics and
theology. This separation continues even into late antiquity, where it
remains rare for scholars working on Prudentius, say, to know
Ambrose's prose and poetry, or for classicists, who would expect a
knowledge of Stoicism to inform their readings of Latin literature, to
delve into workings of theology, the dominant intellectual fervour of
the period. The West has traditionally insisted on finding its cultural
origins in the classical past of Greco-Roman antiquity and/or in the

---

[30]See Frederiksen and Ishai (2006), Limor and Stroumsa, eds (1996), Stroumsa (1996),
Nasrallah and Fiorenza, eds (2009), Reinhartz (2001, 2018) and Heschel (2008) for the
climax.
[31]Frederiksen (2018) and especially Frederiksen et al. (2020).
[32]Reinhartz (2001).

Christian past of the early Church (the ideology of such genealogies have been much analysed and much contested of late, of course). In the past, Jews were excluded from the study of both fields; historically, the separation of the two fields has become part of their established authority. For a Jew, to work in either field has thus been viewed as a statement – sometimes aggressive, sometimes disavowed – of how to relate to such cultural privilege, from elsewhere. To claim a place of belonging on the cultural map: 'those sources belong to me as well'.[33] The contrast between classics and theology, when it comes to confessional positionality, is revealing about both disciplines. According to these disciplinary dynamics, a proper classicist *should* avoid confessional statements altogether. And for a *Jewish* classicist? Must a successful embedding in cultural privilege mean *not to be recognized* as a Jewish classicist?

Underlying these five general frameworks is the foundational question, so provocative for modern politics, of what Judaism is. It is not simply a racial category, although Jews have historically been subject to the foulest racism. Even if one accepted the modern category of race as being useful or determinative, rather than destructive and misleading, there are Jews of all colours, many nationalities, and hugely varied cultures and languages: African, Asian, Chinese, South American, European, Arab . . . They do not conform, that is, to national or racist/racial categories, for all that racists have tried so hard to make them do so. (Here we should mark the possibility of a much longer discussion of purity [*Reinheit*] and its rhetorical function in racial prejudice.)[34] Nor is Judaism simply a religious marker. Not only are there multiple forms of Judaism, from the broad categories of Ashkenazi and Sephardi down to fiercely held local customs, along

[33]Baumgarten (2010: 217).
[34]Starting from Young (1990), Bhaba (1990) and McClintock (1995).

with the transformative ruptures of a long history that separates modern from ancient Jews, but also there are many people who are identified and identify themselves as Jews who deny that they are religious at all or that religion plays any role in their (self-)identification. But nor is Judaism simply a cultural heritage, although there are those who actively identify themselves as 'cultural Jews'.

It is telling, therefore, how often Jews are treated to the word 'extraction': 'she is of Jewish extraction' ('from a Jewish family', 'a Jewish background'). Such terminology is not applied to feminists, people of colour, Christians, Muslims, French citizens ... In modern usage, 'extraction' is used only when there is an anxiety about placement, when there is a sense of being out of place. It makes no sense to say 'a worker of Polish extraction' in Poland: in Poland one says simply 'a worker' or 'a Polish worker'. A 'worker of Polish extraction' is used in countries other than Poland to indicate that the worker, whatever her current citizenship, is descended from Poles, often with the assumption of immigration. It is a way of marking difference, politely but insidiously. It is a way of saying not quite Polish and not quite one of us. It is applied promiscuously to Jews, however. It marks not just descent – from a Jewish family – but also a question of *how* Jewish a person is to be called. Why not just 'she is Jewish' or 'a Jew' rather than 'of Jewish extraction'? Is it that in the rhetoric of identification, the wandering Jew, that old enacted slur, is always out of place, forever homeless? Is it that the speaker of such language is trying to indicate cautious hesitation about naming another's Jewishness – perhaps in embarrassed response to the history of aggressive name-calling? Extraction, however, brings the sense of a certain remove: something has been taken out. It suggests that the person is not fully, really, wholly a Jew, a Jew at home in her Jewishness. It is a phrase that marks the political tensions of naming a Jew a Jew.

The paradox, thus, could be summarized like this. It seems clear enough that 'being Jewish' has a long history of prejudice, exclusion and violence, which in the nineteenth and twentieth centuries included aggressive strategies of making Jewishness visible, with consequent responses of passing and concealment – or vibrant display. In discourses of racism, political belonging, social exclusion, religious commitment, 'being Jewish' has played a repeated and violent rhetorical and consequential role. Jewish communities have maintained a strong if contested and multiple voice of collectivity, and Jewish intellectual, religious and cultural achievements are celebrated as such. In the current politics of identity – itself a contested term, and especially ill-considered if it is taken to assume a single, unified and constant definition of a person: nobody is only Jewish – 'being Jewish' has purchase as a sign of affiliation to a group with a history and a pattern of self-recognition: a means of identification both internally within a group and externally from outside the group, with all the conflicted dynamics of contemporary anxieties about belonging. Yet, even and especially within current arguments about the situatedness of scholarship, there has been remarkably little consideration of what it might mean to label a scholar a 'Jewish classicist', and a certain bafflement about what it would mean to bring together the identities of 'being Jewish' and 'being a classicist'. There are lobbies (volumes, journal issues, websites) for queer classicists, Asian classicists, Black classicists, feminist classicists, Marxist classicists; but not for Jewish classicists. The paradox is that 'being Jewish' has all the attributes of a significant identification – to simplify: a minority with a history of oppression and a strong sense of self-recognition as a group – and yet does not function as such within the politics of the academy. Why, for whom, when and how does this 'identity' of 'Jewish classicist' matter, when it comes to the personal politics of academic work? If it is *not* to matter, why not?

ii Character-building

Where, then, is Jewishness to be located? Let us look first and only most briefly at the cases of four celebrated Jewish scholars of antiquity, now all dead, who lived either side of the Second World War and were influenced profoundly by its political upheavals. Gordon Williams, as cited earlier, indicated that for Eduard Fraenkel, all traces of Jewishness had been extracted from 'his personality'. Early in his career, Fraenkel had apparently been accused publicly in a faculty meeting of being *ein frecher Judenjunge*, ('upstart Jew-boy'?), though this seems to say more about the speaker than Fraenkel (though the fact that it was remembered is also significant).[35] But what would be the signs of Jewishness in a *personality*? A Jewish '*character*'? ('Character' was a code word used in American university admissions systems to keep out Jews and maintain the privilege of the privileged.)[36] Fraenkel's performance of the role of Prussian professor even and especially in exile, matched, as Jas Elsner has noted, by Fraenkel's interest in appearing a 'gentleman' in England (notwithstanding his now well-publicized history of sexual harassment), is set against an imagined and dismissed alternative of his 'Jewishness'.[37] Fraenkel's own self-formation seems to have required an extraction from his family's past – and a bitterness towards this past (which his obituarist tries for his part to qualify as irony, 'perhaps'): certainly not at home with Jewishness. Yet – needless to say? – Gordon Williams does not specify what the signs of a Jewish 'personality' would have been. There are many deeply unpleasant examples, especially from the nineteenth

---

[35]The story is in Williams (1970).
[36]Karabel (2005) and Oren ([1985] 2001). 'A highly subjective evaluation of personality' (Oren [1985] 2001: 196) was crucial through the 1950s to maintaining a quota limiting Jewish admission to Yale, where Williams taught.
[37]Elsner (2021).

century, that could fill this silence with specific imagined traits.[38] 'Character-building,' one aim of the *Bildung* of the Humboldtian university, reveals its more dodgy normativity when it turns to such stereotyping. Fraenkel, in Williams' complicit account, did not wish to be recognized as Jewish. Williams expects you to know what he means. (Do I need to point out that this is how racism functions, especially in polite society?) The oldest of my four examples, and deeply embedded within the hostile and fiercely policed world of Prussian academia, Fraenkel demonstrates what contemporary scholars of racism will see as a thoroughly recognizable pathology of absorbed distaste, aggressively enacted, for the contingency of his own origin.

Unlike Fraenkel, Moses Finley had received some Jewish education as a child (he was a prodigy, who graduated in psychology from Syracuse University at 15 and went immediately, at an 'absurdly young'[39] age, to graduate school first in law, at Columbia University in New York).[40] He grew up in a Conservative – not Orthodox – Jewish community and moved into a world of left-wing, intellectual, immigrant families in and around New York, but came from an already assimilated, bourgeois professional family. It was a shared family decision to change their name from Finkelstein to Finley. He was fired from Rutgers because of his communist views, and came to work, finally, as the Professor of Ancient History at the University of

---

[38]Momigliano (1971; and 1994b: 213) lauded Fraenkel as an archetypal *yeshiva bocher*, on which Horsfall (1990: 63) comments: 'Momigliano's interpretation of Fraenkel as an essentially Jewish teacher is deeply perverse and unconvincing,' while Stray (2014: 154) comments on Brink and Fraenkel: 'Interest in assimilation of one culture by another was provoked by their families' assimilation as German Jews.' How Jewish Fraenkel is/not remains a question . . .

[39]Schwartz (2013: 44), the same age as Badian went to university in New Zealand: Harris (2017: 3).

[40]Best discussion is Schwartz (2013); see also the (other) essays in Harris, ed. (2013) and Jew, Osborne and Scott, eds (2016), especially the contribution by Daniel Tompkins following from Tompkins (2006).

Cambridge. Finley, despite his voluminous work on the ancient Mediterranean, apart from one early introduction to a translation of Josephus, never worked on any aspects of Jewish history in the Roman Empire, and was well known for a studious avoidance of any discussion of his own past. Finley 'embodied a process – the consignment of the Jewish past, in both personal and intellectual senses, to oblivion – which in Europe belonged more to the nineteenth century'[41] – and reflected his communist secularism. His own family had a distinguished rabbinical genealogy, about which he could apparently joke with his closest friends: but both from his view of the ancient Mediterranean and from his own self-presentation, any display of Jewishness was significantly *extracted*. Finley, a heroic class-warrior, who insisted on a political understanding of history, nonetheless found little place for the politics of Judaism in antiquity or in modernity – or for himself within such politics.

Finley's friend, Arnaldo Momigliano, by contrast, lamented Finley's disengagement from Judaism.[42] Momigliano had been a member of the Fascist Party in Italy (a far less surprising affiliation for an Italian Jew than for a German Jew).[43] He failed to gain exemption from the Aryan Laws, however, and left for England where he was appointed as professor at University College London; he also taught regularly at Chicago and Pisa. His parents, however, like Vidal-Naquet's, were murdered by the 'insane racial hatred' of the Nazis, as the epitaph for Momigliano's own gravestone recorded.[44]

Unlike Fraenkel's practice and Finley's predilection, Momigliano wrote on Jews, ancient and modern (as the title of one of his collections

---

[41]Schwartz (2013: 47).
[42]Garnsey (2016); see also Brown (1988) for a longer narrative, and Grafton (2007, reprised in Grafton, 2020).
[43]Stille (1991) is a wonderful account of such a story.
[44]Bowersock (1991: 36).

has it). He knew Hebrew and had studied eclectically in rabbinic sources as a young man: he was proud of the Orthodox home he grew up in. He studied Jewish history, and Jewish scholars, and, in one particularly provocative speculation, argued that the important historiographic formulations of the great nineteenth-century German historian of antiquity, August Gustav Droysen, who invented the word 'Hellenistic' as a technical term for the period of history between Alexander the Great's death and the death of Cleopatra, were influenced by his feelings towards converted Jewish members of the intellectual circles in which he moved.[45] Droysen was great friends with the composer Felix Mendelssohn and numismatist and historian Gottlieb Friedländer, who were at the centre of a community of Jewish intellectuals who had converted to Christianity. In this circle, argues Momigliano, there was a taboo that demanded silence about their Jewish origins. Droysen, a committed Lutheran, who was trying to explain the (providential) roots of Christianity, and who had become – almost against himself – interested in the Jewish foundations of Christianity, nonetheless veered away from completing his researches into Hellenistic Jewish literature, and never finished the book on it he had started. This silence, which for Momigliano needed explanation, was formed, Momigliano argues, on the model of – and out of respect for – Droysen's converted Jewish cadre of friends and colleagues. Momigliano also criticized Marcel Mauss, the anthropologist, who, like Durkheim, was also a Jew, for ignoring the Jewish tradition and specifically the biblical sources, in his influential discussion of the category of the person. Momigliano himself became increasingly fascinated with the problem that he saw at the heart of both Droysen's and Mauss' work – the development of religion and the notion of the person. His interest in the genres of ancient biography and

---

[45]Momigliano (1994a: 147–61. See Stroumsa (2007) and Idel (2007).

autobiography overlapped both with his analysis of the personal politics of individual scholars – how their lives affected their scholarship – and his own increasing autobiographical urge.

Glen Bowersock – using Momigliano's own approach of using a life story to situate a scholar's scholarship – acerbically concludes that Momigliano's historiographical research into the person turned out to be all about himself: he saw Droysen, Mauss and, least persuasively, Ronald Syme, as facing the problems that he himself faced of understanding his own positionality between classicism, Judaism and an Italian, Christian nationhood. 'Momigliano's quest for the person' proved to be 'a quest for one particular person. That was himself.'[46] Momigliano keenly recognizes and discusses his own Jewishness, and its relationship to his commitment to scholarship as a discourse of factual, historical truth, as well as the tensions with classicism and Italian citizenship his own life embodied: he saw himself as 'the *apikoros*, the intellectual heretic' who was, nonetheless, passionately committed to tradition.[47] (*Apikoros*, the standard term for 'heretic' is a corruption of 'Epicurus' – Epicurean: to be a Jewish heretic is to speak Greek.) Momigliano writes about how scholars, Jewish or Christian, conceal Jewish sources and enact a speaking silence about Judaism. In turn, Momigliano is seen by Bowersock as expressing himself, in a way that is concealed to himself. In this overlap between Momigliano's search for self-understanding and his practice of historiography – his insistence on the situatedness of scholarship – we can find one model of what might be meant by a Jewish classicist.

Pierre Vidal-Naquet lived through the end of the Second World War as a child waiting, concealed, for his parents to return.[48] He was

---

[46]Bowersock (1991: 36). See also Clemente (2009).

[47]Stroumsa (2007: 293).

[48]What follows is based on Vidal-Naquet (1995, 1998), Dosse (2020) and the appreciations of Hartog, Schmidt-Pantel and Schnapp, eds (1998) and Hartog (2007); with the general background of Delacroix, Dosse and Garcia, eds (2004) and Leonard (2005).

born in Paris in 1930, but his family for many generations had roots
in the long-established Jewish community of southern France. It was
a bourgeois, successful, assimilated family – his father a lawyer of
some standing. He could say, as Claude Lévi-Strauss writes, 'Culture
was paramount in my milieu. *This is what was sacred.*'[49] He was deeply
embedded in an intellectual community: his cousins were the future
classicists, Claude Mossé and Jacques Brunschwig; he was friends at
school with the historian Pierre Nora; he worked with Jean Bollack
(who could easily have been chosen among my test cases of Jewish
Classicists); made friends with Arno Mayer at Princeton, and was
deeply influenced by and became friends with Moses Finley and
Arnaldo Momigliano (every figure in this network is Jewish). It is
telling, however, that Dreyfus is mentioned on the first page of Vidal-
Naquet's autobiography. Fraenkel, Finley and Momigliano were all
forced into exile by the politics of the day; Vidal-Naquet's family was
shattered by the war, and his career defined by the Algerian War and
his political engagement with Holocaust deniers. For Vidal-Naquet, to
be a historian, with a commitment to truth and justice, is a vocation
for which his own sense of living in and through the violent injustices
of history is determinative. Dreyfus haunts French Jewish self-
understanding and Vidal-Naquet calls his own political passion 'une
obsession dreyfusarde' (his father has explained the case to him as a
child).[50] 'In my academic work,' he writes, 'the theme of doubling plays
a role of such importance'[51] – referring to his interest in ideas of self
and other, the opposition of Athens and Sparta, or the doubling of

---

[49]Loyer ([2015] 2018: 41), Lévi-Strauss's biographer, contrasts this with what she calls, 'the
cold and desiccated character of Judaism', shamefully and unthinkingly reproducing
Christian slurs from the Reformation onwards.
[50]For the connection between the Dreyfus Affair and the history of scholarship, see Stroumsa
(2021).
[51]Vidal-Naquet (1995: 164).

mythological figuration; or, as his student, François Hartog puts it, his double role as historian of reality, historian of the imaginary.[52] Yet, this sense of doubling doubles as elements of his life and scholarship overlap. He sums up his career like this:

> It is also that, a historian of the Greeks, a historian of contemporary crises and crimes, I became a historian of the Jews; not double, simply, if I can put it like this, but triple and even quadruple, if you add this other aspect of my work: the history of history. This is not an easy condition to live but I try to live it effectively in all its complexity.[53]

Like Finley, he was asked to write the introduction to a translation of Josephus;[54] unlike Finley – and the contrast is striking –– for Vidal-Naquet this commission led to a career as a Jewish historian, ancient and modern. For Vidal-Naquet there exists 'a certain solidarity-rivalry' between Jews and Greeks: he quotes approvingly Elias Bickerman, another influential Jewish historian of the Jews: 'The Jews became the people of the book when that book was translated into Greek.'[55] Like Momigliano, then, it would seem, Vidal-Naquet is a Jew who not only writes about the history of both the Jews and the Greeks, but also writes about historiography and its silences and lies about Jewish experience, and sees Jews and Greeks as conceptually linked. For him, there is a complex continuity between his work on holocaust deniers, torture and the Algerian war, the history of Jews, the history of historiography, and Greek history. Yet, unlike Momigliano, Vidal-Naquet did not come from a religious household, to the extent that he was not even

---

[52]Hartog (2007: 55). Hartog, too, writes a study of Dreyfus (Hartog 2017).

[53]Vidal-Naquet (1995: 290–1).

[54]Momigliano (1994b) reviews this, with reference to Finley – continuing the network.

[55]Vidal-Naquet (1995: 291). On Bickerman, see Baumgarten (2010, and especially 193–205; with Momigliano 1994b: 217–21) on *his* long friendship with Momigliano; and Manning, ed. (2010).

circumcised. (Lévi-Strauss, who had a vexed relation with the religion of his grandfather, a rabbi, when asked if he had circumcised his children, replied that they were 'both circumcised, by accident' – a hilarious disavowal, not least for an anthropologist who might be thought to be more aware of the power of such a defining ritual of the body. By accident?!)[56] Vidal-Naquet married a non-Jewish woman (to his family's mild consternation) and his children are baptized. History, he says, 'was my passion, if you like, my religion': 'for me, an atheist, history was the only possible substitute for religion'.[57] (As Yerushalmi diagnosed, history is the faith of fallen Jews.)[58] In response to Sartre's *Reflections on the Jewish Question*, Vidal-Naquet writes – with whatever pleasure in the ironies of disavowal – 'For my part, I rank myself, without hesitation, among the "inauthentic" Jews.'[59] For all his claims that his work is integrated and, indeed, a way of life, Vidal-Naquet, whose home was destroyed by the Nazis, remains not quite at home in his Judaism. Identity remains coloured by anxiety about authenticity – a continuing question of what it might mean to be a Jew, a real Jew, a Jew really. *Laïcité* is a necessary frame for a French Jewish classicist.

These four distinguished academics, each passionate and articulate about the ideals of their profession, were each profoundly marked by the war and its politics: three went into exile in England – with their different responses to such a condition – and Vidal-Naquet, the fourth, was deracinated and moved from family to family. Each of the three lived the double life of an exile – aware of the life left behind and the

---

[56]As many of the first generation of anthropologists had evangelical Christian parents, (Larsen 2014), so there is an interesting history of Jewish anthropologists/sociologists and their families (Lévi-Strauss, Durkheim, Mauss, Fortes, Boas . . .).

[57]Vidal-Naquet (1998: 19; and Vidal-Naquet 2004: 20).

[58]See Yerushalmi (1982). Howard (2009) is more robust, if less directly apposite, than Myers (2002); see also Idel (2007). Momigliano (1994b: 169) writes of Bernays: 'Having received a faith, he did not have to look to history for one.'

[59]Vidal-Naquet (1995: 167).

stark contrast with their new environment; and the narrative of each within the institutional history of the field is precisely as masterly figures who translated knowledge from one intellectual environment to another: paradigmatically, Fraenkel 'brought German scholarly methods and standards to Oxford'. The institutional success of each man as an outsider – a foreigner as well as a go-between – was repeatedly noted as a rarity, and each performed that role with gusto. Yet, doubleness runs through these biographies in a different way also. Each account is concerned with concealment, revelation and untold stories. Fraenkel's intense denial of signs of Jewishness; Finley's refusal to speak of his past (especially marked in a historian); Momigliano's intellectual pursuit of unexplained silences and hidden engagements with Jewish narratives; Vidal-Naquet's public fight against Holocaust deniers, his childhood amid increasingly vitriolic anti-Semitism. Speaking out and speaking silences ... Each of the four was passionate about a self-placement in history – about the continuities over time and the connection of past and present. Fraenkel's *magnum opus* of his time in Oxford, his commentary on the *Agamemnon*, set out to be comprehensive in its recognition of past scholarship and, consequently, of Fraenkel's own hard-won place in the roster of great scholars, like Odysseus among the dead heroes in the Underworld. Finley and Momigliano wrote repeatedly of problems 'ancient and modern', and Momigliano extended his critical eye to the impact of the life stories of modern historians on their historiography. Both insisted on the mutual impact of antiquity and modernity, the power of antiquity in the present. Vidal-Naquet, even more so, was instrumentally engaged with modern French crises and saw these politically engaged interventions in a line with his ancient studies and his concern for what history writing should be. Marked in their lives by the violence of contemporary politics, each professed that a responsibility to truth through understanding the past and through a vigilance about method was essential to the profession of a scholar.

Each maintained such principles fiercely (inevitably to the fear of some of their colleagues). Yet the range of responses to their status as Jews runs through the different and shifting positions of Fraenkel's concealment, Finley's silence, Momigliano's obsessive recalibration and Vidal-Naquet's authoritatively proclaimed inauthenticity (strategies of doubleness, each). None is simply at home in their Jewishness as an identity, even as – perhaps because – each was compelled by the politics of the day into being forcibly interpellated as Jewish.

I have offered here four snapshots of leading Jewish classicists who lived through the transformative events of the Second World War, a German, an American, an Italian, a Frenchman – and, for reasons of space, these can be no more than snapshots: intellectual, social, personal, political networks, formative of identity, could be extended *ad libitum,* and, of course, many other examples could have been chosen (Friedrich Solmsen, Elias Bickerman, Margarete Bieber, Paul Friedländer, Martin Ostwald, or Thomas Rosenmeyer, say, in the USA, or, for non-exiles, Moses Hadas, Louis Feldman, Meyer Reinhold; in England, David Lewis or Victor Ehrenberg (with his son, the British constitutional historian and Regius Professor at Cambridge, Sir Geoffrey Elton, a more assimilable name); in France, Jean Bollack or Jacqueline de Romilly, who, baptized in 1940, converted to Catholicism on her deathbed. (Or the complex cases of Felix Jacoby, who had converted to Protestantism, but, nonetheless, under Nazi race laws was banned as a Jew and joined Fraenkel in Oxford; or Werner Jaeger,[60]

---

[60]Jacoby wrote to Enoch Powell in June, 1939: 'Somebody told me that you had a somewhat strong antisemitic bias. Now I am no friend of the Jews on the whole, and I have only few and not very intimate relations with them. But as things now are in Germany, although I cannot change my feelings, I try now to repress them'. The case of Jaeger has been studied, in particular: see Elsner (2013) and Calder, ed. (1992). On Rosenmeyer, MacDonald (2007) which I discussed with Patricia Rosenmeyer; on Ostwald, Aciman (2016) and Ostwald (2010). Other references are given below.

who worked with the Nazi education ministry, but left for England and then America because of his Jewish wife: Paul Friedländer bitterly spotted the Nazi, still, in Jaeger . . .).[61] There was no Jew tenured in any American classics department in Greek before 1930, and only one in Latin, who rapidly became a high-level administrator:[62] the refugees broke the glass ceiling, but not for women. If we widened the scope to include equally influential figures who worked primarily in other fields but with an interest in antiquity, we could redress the gender balance a little with a political scientist such as Hannah Arendt, or the founder of the Thames and Hudson publishing house, Eva Neurath, although the list of exiled academics inevitably reflects the gender expectations of the era.[63] For women, things changed far more slowly. Anne Lebeck, who took her own life at the age of only 37 in 1973, after being offered a tenured position at Chicago, was by all accounts a strikingly, even frighteningly smart and intense scholar, who came to New York first to train as an actor and dancer before discovering the wonder of Greek literature, but she is in one respect at least typical of the 1960s, the years in which she became a classicist: her Jewish background – her parents owned a store in Nashville – was not

---

[61]On Friedländer on Jaeger see Calder and Braun (1996), who list but do not discuss Friedländer's annotations on *Paideia* with any purchase.

[62]This one exception was Monroe Deutsch (1879–1955), Vice President and Provost at the University of California (born and bred in Los Angeles). In 1941, he published *Our Legacy of Religious Freedom*, a passionate defence of the history of American religious toleration, in which he also noted (16) the 'burning coals of intolerance lying just beneath the placid surface' of American life.

[63]See Häntzschel (2001), who explains why Calder (1992) finds only 1 woman in his 18 most influential immigrant classical scholars. Coser allows 3 women in his 48 test cases. Both Calder and Coser are strikingly direct and frank about 'virulent' (Coser 1984: 7) American anti-Semitism in this era. See Hallett (2019) on the Society for Classical Studies and access. The literature on the influence of émigré scholars on British and American culture is immense. Snowman (2002), my cousin, is a starting point. A small redress of the gender balance in Hallett (2018). No female immigrant classicist held a tenured university position. On classicist exiles in Britain – no women – see Wasserstein (2005).

mentioned. This decade was still an era of passing, though it was, as Dan Tompkins glossed her personal story, a time 'when it was all cracking open'. So, Carl Bridenbaugh, the President of the American Historical Association, in his presidential address of 1962, could lament the presence of students of 'lower middle-class or foreign origin' in the field – because 'their emotions frequently get in the way': his language is not subtly coded – but, by the end of the decade, such remarks would look like a relic of a deservedly lost past.[64] Bridenbaugh's address was a melancholic lament for the loss of an old-style of historical awareness – but, within his own lifetime, he came to embody a consciously transcended era.

In particular, however, Erich Auerbach, German exile, writing through the war in Istanbul of Odysseus' return to his home, has become a telling figure for a specifically exilic, Jewish philology, not least for James Porter, Jewish philologist[65] – looking longingly, like Judah Halevi, to the East from the furthest West – just as Daniel Mendelssohn, whose life-writing has dramatized his Odyssean journey as a classicist around his Jewish family, has also returned to the figure of the philologist in Auerbach:[66] Mendelssohn, whose own name could take us back to the iconic figure of the Jew finding a place in the Enlightenment classical tradition, Moses Mendelssohn,[67] in the title and subject of his reflections on Auerbach evokes W. G. Sebald – which would take us back to Sebald's friend and muse, Martin Ostwald[68] ... who, like Auerbach, strived to embody the classical

[64]Thanks to Dan Tompkins, Seth Schein and David Konstan for sharing reminiscences of the charismatic Lebeck. Bridenbaugh (1963: 317), discussed by Palmer (2014); and Brown (2008: 254–5 n. 23).
[65]Porter (2008, 2010, 2017). See also Boyarin (2015).
[66]Mendelsohn (2020).
[67]Leonard (2012).
[68]Aciman (2016) for Sebald and Ostwald.

tradition that the violence of his times threatened to destroy.[69] Looking back to an imagined Europe ... Yet, from such a wealth of examples, these four snapshots will have to suffice to provide an exemplary framework, perhaps a perspective on a generation, that can act as an introduction to a more contemporary view. How, then, has 'being a Jewish classicist' changed?

iii Let me tell you a story

There is a marvellous television show called 'Old Jews Telling Jokes', which consists of no more than a series of elderly Jews telling their favourite jokes to camera. It makes me wish that I could begin here by playing a movie of at least some of the forty hours and more of Zoom and in person conversations I participated in with young and old Jewish classicists, talking of what being Jewish means to them as a scholar. The interviews were full of jokes, moving personal stories, contradictions, dissimulations, revelations, embarrassment, and wonderfully involuted, engaged and dismissive reflections on the question of 'how Jewish'. Inevitably, the full richness of such material has to be sacrificed to produce a narrative – along with the dictates of reasonable discretion that always plays a role in contemporary oral history.

The sample was chosen with the aim of producing a range of gender, institution, nationality, career track and age. Thus, the list includes scholars working in or originating from at least ten different countries/nationalities (England, France, Germany, Holland, India, Israel, Italy, Palestine, Switzerland, USA), ranging from graduates who have not yet finished their dissertations, to early and mid-career

---

[69]Ostwald (2010).

scholars, to distinguished emeriti (ages 28–87). Although I have set up this chapter as a contrast between the generation who lived through the war and a contemporary generation, there is always a significant overlap between age groups, and academia is one arena where the different age groups significantly interact: as a student, I met Finley and Vidal-Naquet, and many of the interviews reverted to recalling networks of scholars and significant meetings across countries and age ranges. The roster of interviews includes academics who identify as literary scholars, ancient historians, including epigraphers, philosophers, intellectual historians and art historians, along with theologians and historians of religion in antiquity who are not in departments of classics. Reflections from Muslim scholars who work on Judaism, and from other classicists involved in contemporary politics of the discipline, but who are not Jewish, were also canvassed to provide a richer comparative frame. All were made aware of the project in agreeing to talk.

The methodology adopted was a standard semi-structured interview model: a list of the same basic questions, extended by the contingencies of each life-story or discussion, including looping back to repetitions of the initial questions in the light of subsequent answers. I have tried in the account that follows to expand beyond the anecdotal – despite the love of the anecdote that every interviewee revelled in – and to develop some general frameworks for discussion. Where named, each scholar has agreed to such exposure: whatever the theory of situatedness, talking about colleagues' personal lives, and by name, must always invoke taboos, but as a key theme of this paper is concealment and revelation of identity, *not* to name seemed to rehearse the theme too embarrassedly. For those who feel underrepresented (underexposed?), well, over to you to continue the story. Reflections on one's own life, experiences and careers are a form of discourse where the narrative of '*wie es eigentlich gewesen*' and the projections of imagination, desire and the vagaries of memory are intimately intertwined and often mutually exclusive. Such story-telling is a crucial factor in the construction of what it means to be a Jewish classicist. There is a continuum between the obituaries, histories, biographies and autobiographies I have begun with, and the anecdotes I elicited – the material for future writing, future memorial, future self-understanding. What I am seeking to explore here is not so much the sociology or history of academic institutions (there has, of course, been fine work on the inclusion and exclusion of minorities into the university system),[70] nor the actor networks of contemporary scholarship, nor a list of Jewish scholars. Rather, my aim is to explore the discursive construction of self-awareness and the performance of the politics of identity involved in asking: 'What is a Jewish Classicist?'

Glenn Most summed up one particular strand of conversation in his typically incisive and forthright manner when he replied immediately to me that the fact of his being born into a Jewish family had no more effect on his scholarship than the fact of his height. 'I do not have an ounce of religiosity in me,' he wrote, indicating he would talk to me not out of any interest in the topic but out of friendship. He managed, nonetheless, to continue to explain his lack of interest for over 80 minutes. The suggestion that values of philological scholarship trump and should trump any personal, religious or emotional deformation is a scholarly trope, and, indeed, a precious value of the community, which contemporary arguments about the significance of situatedness have not shifted. To enter the academy demands hard work, and complicity with its models, and brings its rewards. Jean Bollack turned to the principles of German philology in the same

---

[70]See, from a very large bibliography, specifically on Jews, Oren ([1985] 2001), Klingenstein (1991) and Karabel (2005); on race, Ahmed (2012) and Wilder (2013); on immigrants, Coser (1984) and Crawford, Ulmschneider and Elsner, eds (2017); on class, Hall and Stead (2020) and Richardson (2013).

spirit, though it became harder to maintain such critical distance when he turned to write about Paul Celan's poetry, as he did with such distinction.[71] This privileging of objective scholarship has a long history, of course, and is not the same thing as not having a sense of oneself as a Jew – although being Jewish has often been regarded as an adequate reason for exclusion from the hallowed groves. (Martin Ostwald, the most kindly man, when an aunt asked why he didn't study Jews rather than Greeks, exploded, 'The Greeks are rational!' When he got to England in 1938, though, he had said he wanted to become a rabbi, since he was barred from university in Germany, a plan he never enacted: desperate times, desperate measures; Thomas Rosenmeyer trained as a piano tuner.)[72] Alan Bowman, who comes from a fiercely secular, communist family, a background Mary Jacobus would recognize, agreed with this principle and saw nothing Jewish in his own scholarship. When I asked him about his role as Senior Censor of Christ Church (the head of the institution), he confessed that before taking up the role, he had been asked about his religious commitments – Christ Church has, after all, what is a cathedral. He had indicated that he would read lessons for the alumni events only from the Old Testament. In a perfect parody of Orwell's famous parody, he agreed – laughing – that while he believed in nothing, he didn't believe in some things more strongly than others.

More tellingly, one feminist, observant, Jewish scholar of the Hebrew Bible, Hindy Najman, described with forceful lyricism how

---

[71]Simon-Nahum (2010), also (2014).

[72]Chopp (2010) and Ostwald (2010: 61). For the politics of Ostwald's kindliness, see Aciman (2016), who emphasizes Ostwald's desire to build back bridges with Germany. Ostwald's memoirs (2010) mention his shock at brief encounters with American anti-Semitism, especially from Gilbert Highet, and celebrate his own Jewish family life, but, unlike Vidal-Naquet, make no connection between his love of civilization, history writing, and a desire for continuity with what was taken from him in 1939.

some scholars argued *as Jews*: their love of interpretation and an expansive mode of reasoning, that looked back to the hermeneutics of the Talmud and outwards to the bigger picture of the world gave them in her eyes a distinctive approach that she appreciated profoundly. In this perspective, not all 'Jewish writers' were Jews, and not all Jews were 'Jewish writers'. Yet, when I asked if she taught as a Jew, Hindy Najman replied with immediate scorn: 'No! I am a scholar!' The paradox remained unresolved.

At the other end of the spectrum from Glenn Most, two historians, Jonathan Price in Tel Aviv and David Levene in New York, both accepted the description of 'Jewish classicist' with reflective care. Jonathan Price moved from his country of birth in order to live a more committed Jewish life – he describes himself as a modern Orthodox Jew; David Levene, more conflictedly, as 'traditionally observant', though with demurrals and redefinitions along the way. David Levene told me how he would introduce a class on the history of Roman religion by announcing his partiality as a Jewish reader (to the dismay, he reported, of a colleague).[73] David Levene glossed his style as 'ethical reading', influenced by midrash, something Hindy Najman would recognize, happily. His intention by declaring his own partiality, however, was to encourage his class to think about the positionality of all writers and readers of historiography: the ideological and conflicted authority of writing the past.

Jonathan Price works on Josephus, the multilingual inscriptions of the province of Palestine – but also Thucydides. The link, he explained, was civil war, and, one might add from the subtitle of his book, internal war: Josephus is the most celebrated traitor, who escaped from a suicide pact as a leader of the revolution to write in Rome his histories

---

[73]The colleague, however, convincingly demurred, at length, from this account. Such are the contests of oral history.

of the Jewish Revolt and of Jewish antiquities for a Greek-speaking audience: the go-between or collaborator *par excellence*. The multilingual inscriptions are testimony of a divided imperial culture, where the elite language of Greek, the administrative and army language of Latin and the local Aramaic jostle up against each other as signs and symptoms of the divided and divisive society in conflict with itself and with foreign power.

Both saw studying Jewish history as a topic that they had a specific concern to understand and contribute to, but also saw no difficulty with sharing the material, causal explanations of contemporary historiographical methodology. Their interest was personal, but not, therefore, inevitably compromised. One historian of antiquity I spoke to who was Ultra-Orthodox (Charedi: his own description) was more guarded, but also declared that a scholar 'has a responsibility to produce a consensual discourse with which the academic community can agree'. He had been told, when he gave his first public seminar, by another Jewish scholar who would turn out to be a colleague in later years, that he had 'to choose between wearing a *streimel* and wearing a mortar-board' – which he remembered not as advice or a choice but as a vivid and aggressive demonstration of prejudice. As with the case of Fraenkel, when Jewishness does become a criterion of public debate, rancorousness, it seems, is not far behind: *recognizing* a Jew – from a look, a way of dressing, a way of speaking – reopens the scars of past prejudice, and, like Jewish jokes, opens a tension between insiders and outsiders, with all the dynamics of being in or out of the club. For a Jew – as for any scholar producing a form of national, local, political, self-declared participatory history – to write on the history of the Jews is a self-implicating process, which is part of scholarly methodology to discuss (for all that such a self-aware and self-exposing discussion has all too often been avoided, and not only by Jewish classicists, of course). A female graduate student in Israel – in literary studies – when asked about the perils of self-implication, immediately quipped, 'I am okay, I am not a historian.' The thrust of the answer, to avoid an argument about history which threatens to derail so many debates in Israel, made its point, even if it did no more than deflect the difficulties of the issue.

Molly Myerowitz Levine, at peace with her religiously observant life,[74] while teaching for more than thirty-five years at the traditionally Black university, Howard, recommended a 'dual consciousness': 'to hold two contradictory ideas at the same time', she insisted with a laugh, 'is the mark of an intellectual' – and thus – from the opposite perspective of Glenn Most – saw no salient intellectual category of Jewish classicist.[75] Aaron Kachuk, however, who came to classics from committedly studying Hebrew at Yale because of an initial fascination with Hellenistic Judaism ('came for Philo, stayed for Homer'), described his Princeton professor's distaste when, as a graduate student, he channelled his 'Midrashic anachronic chaos' in writing about classical literature: with performative self-fulfilment, he described the eruption of this 'Jewishness' in his own prose as 'Midrashic profusion, confusion, effusion'. He was willing to describe himself with some passion as a Jewish classicist – but, nonetheless, was distinctly upset when in a lecture a colleague called *another* scholar a 'Jewish classicist'.

James Porter provides a paradigm of a further coordinate on the map. He grew up in New Hampshire, with only a bare Jewish education and active religious life in a Reform community, but, nonetheless, said this experience 'shaped everything I do'. His 'sense of alienation', of 'not belonging' was crucial: Judaism meant little, being Jewish was

---

[74]Her account of the 'peculiarly polite yet inhumane brand of Wellesley anti-Semitism' in the 1960s is both shocking and funny (Levine 1985).

[75]Despite Levine (2018). She was echoing Scott Fitzgerald (rather than the 'impossible things' of *Alice in Wonderland*).

formative. Yet, he never 'felt more Jewish' than when he worked on Nietzsche's philology, living in an apartment block in what had been East Berlin. It fuelled his 'scholarly rage': he was 'enraged, saddened, fascinated' by what he was reading and experiencing, together.[76] Yet, he, too, found it hard to point to *anyone else* who he thought of as a 'Jewish classicist': it wasn't how he categorized the world, although it *was* how he formulated his own self-representation, in quiet anger. His advisers were Martin Ostwald and Thomas Rosenmeyer (who had become close and lasting friends in a British camp for enemy aliens – crucial term – in Canada) but he saw no genealogy there, at least when he was being taught. Like many I interviewed, Porter was explicit that how he now thought about – and publicly expressed – his identity (a term he put in several sets of inverted commas) was not available to him when he was younger. It was weeks after our interview that Porter remembered – eat your heart out, Dr Freud – that as a graduate he had translated two books from German, one on the Final Solution, the other on Martin Luther and anti-Semitism.

The five-year-old Amy Richlin, in Hackensack, New Jersey, stroppily replied to her grandmother's Yiddish delight that she was a 'beautiful little Jewish girl' (*yiddische scheyne meydel*), with 'I am an American girl.' Both her parents, though they grew up poor, knew some Latin; her mother in old age could conjugate verbs even when suffering with dementia. Her father, who was forced to give up his musical training to work as a butcher, rather wonderfully took 'Vercingetorix' as his middle name. Amy Richlin completed the unfulfilled promise of their careers – the classic story of generational social rising, through educational success in classics (already turned tragic by Hardy in *Jude the Obscure*). She threw herself into student life in Princeton with

---

[76]Harriet Fertik also described her self-consciousness as a Jew increasing at being treated as 'a salient curiosity' in Germany.

such verve, that she founded the women's crew (inspired by Thomas Hughes' *Tom Brown at Oxford*, 1861) and even served in chapel. If Amy Richlin, looking backwards, now describes her decision to go into classics as a 'sort of internalised anti-Semitism', for Jim Porter being a classicist had intensified his sense of being Jewish through anti-Semitism. In Britain, well into the 1970s, 'smart boys' – a significant title – were directed into classics as *the* privileged subject: a route into assimilating to an educational and cultural tradition. Being Jewish – which need have no connection to institutional Judaism – and becoming a classicist is a drama of fitting in, of finding a place, whether the drama is disavowed, misrecognized or played to the hilt. Seth Schein, as I mentioned in the introduction, was advised by his professor, Moses Hadas, not to enter the discipline because of its ingrained anti-Semitism (a different sense of tradition was his cultivated explanation) – and when he had taken up a position, found himself introduced to a visitor by Gilbert Highet as 'the cosmopolitan member of the department'.[77] To choose classics turns out to express a sense of belonging or alienation, elsewhere.

Self-description is always in a dynamic tension with how others describe you and are described by you – and with the normative, social expectations involved in such processual constructions of recognition. Several interviewees, when asked about being a Jewish classicist, proceeded to talk first and at length about other people, listing cases they knew – often long dead – or cases they found telling (Froma Zeitlin sent me several lists). To move to a personal, self-reflective narrative was more difficult, and sometimes resisted

---

[77]On Highet, a man of complex self-presentation, see the hagiographic Ball (2021), in which Highet receives laudatory comments from his students, including Froma Zeitlin and David Konstan. Highet had a distinguished war, and is said by Ball to have hated Nazis, but was friends with Jaeger, whose *Paideia* Highet translated. On Jaeger's Nazism, see above 75–6, with n60, n61.

altogether. Is the question, 'What is a Jewish classicist?' about the self or the other? Froma Zeitlin, whose life work could be summed up as the exploration of how projections of the other are part of self-formation, claimed she had never thought of how this might be related to her formative experiences as an outspoken Jewish feminist in Ivy League establishments from the 1960s onwards.[78] The problem was epitomized for me in this vivid and funny exchange. 'The one classical historian who I would definitely describe as Jewish,' said one historian, 'is Erich Gruen.' When I asked Erich Gruen, who became an ancient historian on the advice of Martin Ostwald, he replied by trying out different possibilities. Did he write 'from a Jewish background', 'as a Jew', 'from a Jewish point of view'. He denied them all: 'wrong identity', he concluded. He wrote about Jewish history, but, he insisted, it was a trajectory of his earlier work. I did point out that it was a trajectory that had stopped – perhaps reached home? – he had, after all worked on Jewish stuff, not just history but biblical texts, for decades now.[79] But he was unimpressed by my suggested version of his career, too. It would seem that it is easier to project the category of Jewish classicist onto another scholar than it is to adopt it for oneself.

This shifting between uncertain, qualified or rejected narratives of the self and more willing recognition of others is matched by a refusal of everyone interviewed to imagine any essentialist definition based on blood or birth, as anything other than toxic. The fact that Keith Hopkins and Oliver Taplin both discovered late in life that they were technically (*halachically*) Jewish, makes minimal difference to who they are or to their scholarship – though it does add piquancy to the dramatic symmetry of the era-defining debate about the nature of the

---

[78]See Zeitlin et al. (2019), which is also fascinating on Vernant and Jewishness.
[79]Gruen (2002, 2008, 2010) have been taken by some critics as a significantly and designedly diasporic view of diaspora.

Roman Emperor conducted between Keith Hopkins and Fergus Millar – a debate which so inspired the young Mary Beard:[80] it is an *agon* between a Jew who did not know he was a Jew, and a non-Jew whose wife and children are Jewish, and who described himself as an 'honorary Jew' – elective affiliation versus unaware birthright. A plot for a novel, perhaps, but only a racist would see such facts as determinative or even relevant for the scholarly debate and its impact.

Now, I could turn here to consider the methodological role of the participant observer in anthropological encounters with informants, but it would be wrong to overhype what the stories I have just collected constitute: designedly no more than an edited set of anecdotes shared between friends. (As philologists we should know that the plural of anecdote is not evidence.) Yet, collectively, these stories do reveal some indicative coordinates. First, no one had a glib or worked out answer to the question of what is a Jewish classicist, even though they were primed of the subject beforehand. Certainly, nobody made any suggestion that the mere fact of a bloodline mattered (one sign of the desperate, racist madness for purity). Each person developed stories, backtracked, and changed perspectives as the conversations proceeded: contradictions, jokes, self-mocking, deflections, uncertainties were integral to the definitional discourse, not distractions from it: jokes in particular, Jewish jokes, everywhere. Each person, even when they denied any connection between their Jewishness and their scholarship, recognized that Jewishness played some role in who they were, a recognition sometimes unwillingly pursued, sometimes proclaimed; even the most religiously committed Jews recognized a significant gap between their scholarship and their religious perspective.

For the older scholars, in particular, their self-awareness and willingness to speak out had changed over time. There was little

---

[80]Beard (2019).

deployment of critical secular studies to consider the impact of the
ideology of secularism on the (mis)understanding of religion, nor
reference to its cousin, critical race studies, in the discussion of anti-
Semitism.[81] Nor did anyone speak zealously of guarding Western
civilization, however reflectively they placed themselves with regard
to the past and the discipline's history. In short, the situatedness of the
scholar remained opaque, dissimulated, performed, denied: narrated
but not fully understood, not fully made visible. The partial nature of
such self-understanding and the precarious and contingent narration
of the stories of the self stand in striking tension with the proclamations
of so much contemporary identity politics which demand certainty of
recognition – and often excoriate the weak-hearted. Adorno, not a
scholar with whom I am much in sympathy, is incisive, however, when
he determines that the desire 'to speak as a ...' is a worryingly
authoritarian gesture: 'Transcendent critique sympathizes with
authority in its very form, even before expressing any content: the
expression "as a ... I ..." in which one can insert any orientation, from
dialectical materialism to Protestantism, is symptomatic of that.'[82] The
question, 'What is a Jewish classicist?' did *not* provoke authoritarian
answers but rather an insistence on multiplicity of perspectives and
uncertainty of positionality as a necessary part of a response. This
conclusion, I think, sets a challenging question to current political
rhetoric about positionality and its rather too shrill and certain
epistemology.

National and institutional frameworks produced significant
difference. Two, Orthodox Jewish women in Israel described the

---

[81]See the excellent McCoskey (2012) and the works cited in Salaymeh and Lavi (2021), for
good starts.
[82]Adorno (1993: 194). In the *Dialectic of Enlightenment* (Horkheimer and Adorno [1947]
2002), Adorno writes on Homer with Max Horkheimer, who would lead us back to Finley
(Tompkins 2016).

surprise of the students that they – as Orthodox women – could possibly have been taught Greek. 'Regarded as the enemy,' was one, wry and immediately qualified description of her reception as a scholar of Greek in her politically charged educational environment (she immediately added that all the students, if not their parents, knew the *Percy Jackson* movies . . .). Each French scholar, as already indicated, politicized their stories in a line from Dreyfus, through the Shoah/ Vichy to Algeria, with a focus on *laïcité* – a very different account of historical self-understanding from the British. None of the Americans cared to reflect deeply on a history that involved exclusionary quotas for Jewish students in some Ivy League universities into the 1960s and even the 1970s. That was then . . . Stephen Greenblatt, however, who has written so instructively about Lucretius in the Renaissance, told me with some relish that when he was an undergraduate at Yale in the early 1960s, he was taken on by his professor as an assistant and thus sent to the Finance Office for a scholarship to fund this work. The Finance Officer looked at his name and asked if he was Jewish, and declared that too many Jews were applying for financial aid. Just as the government had statistics to prove the criminal tendency of Sicilians, he said, Yale had statistics that showed too many Jews were asking for money. (Yale, for years, had a particular track record with such administrative and social nastiness.)

It was striking, however, how many Jewish scholars, especially women, also saw their work as motivated by a concern for social justice. For the scholars of antiquity I interviewed, anti-Semitism became a passionately experienced force – rather than a low-level expectation – only in theology (or, occasionally, abroad). In theology, shocking stories emerged of anti-Semitic tropes being aggressively and publicly deployed, especially where early Christianity was concerned. At a conference, Paula Frederiksen was accused by a distinguished male professor of trying to reclaim Jesus for Judaism (as if there was any doubt that Jesus was Jewish): 'What would I do with him?' she replied, in hilarious bafflement. Hindy Najman recalled her shock that her colleague, the (Protestant) Regius Professor of Hebrew at Oxford, at a conference tried to explain why Jews are hated – with the apparently unrecognized anti-Semitic trope, 'Jews think they are the Chosen People.' (The gender dynamics of these cases also should not be ignored.) The anti-Jewish rhetoric of the texts of early Christianity has left its mark. The teleology of defining the field as 'early Christianity' has its ongoing consequences.

The public (in)-visibility of Jewishness – a major difference, historically and now, with the enactment of racial prejudice against people of colour – resulted, as we mentioned earlier, in strategies of exposure: the invention of a racist physiognomics, the insistence that Jews sounded or smelled different, the markers of yellow stars, the architectural force of the ghetto. I was told many versions of 'funny, he didn't look Jewish' stories, along with their reflex in the discomfort of remembered anti-Semitic 'casual comments'. This question of (in)-visibility also has resulted in historically specific strategies of passing – though passing is shared with all forms of prejudice, including colonialism – and specific dynamics of silence and speaking out (as well as demonstrations of resistance, especially by Charedi groups, who dress *to be recognized* in public).[83] Our long conversations about 'how Jewish' reflect this history: it changes how stories are told and exchanged. 'How Jewish?' is not just a question but also a performance. This for me was epitomized in a subsidiary question of why Jews were not considered a minority in terms of political lobbying or educational policy. In England, there are just under 300,000 Jews: this barely

---

[83]Ernst Badian, Harvard University's finest, purchased used rabbinical vestments from Eastern Europe to wear in synagogue in Quincy, Boston, a performance if ever there was one.

registers against 3.4 million Muslims, and over 1 million Hindus. In
Britain, there are significantly more Sikhs or Chinese than Jews. Jews
also have a long history of prejudice against them, institutionally and
violently on the streets. So, why not a minority? A standard answer I
garnered from non-Jews was, 'Because Jews are so rich and successful'
– a standard anti-Semitic trope, alas. Yet, answers from Jews also
refused the categorization ('A minority? Me?!') – but from a double
motivation: partly shared pride in achievement beyond statistical
norms, but partly an anxiety about standing out and being recognized
– an unwillingness to be singled out as Jewish from the outside.
Against dominant and domineering attempts to insist on difference,
fitting in has been absorbed as an aim and achievement. The politics
of this belonging becomes more complex and disturbing, however,
when 'how Jewish?' therefore also becomes 'how white?'[84]

'Exceptionalism' bedevils classics and its genealogies of privilege.
My story here of 'the Jewish reception of classics', in contrast, has
been about the varied embedding of Jewish classicists in institutions,
national histories and personal narratives, and, above all, about
how the question, 'What is a Jewish classicist?' prompts stories,
jokes, misprisions, disagreements, disavowals: a contingent, shifting,
narrativization of cultural identity, performed through the exchange
of tales and other informal discursive forms in the processual
exploration of recognition. These stories are informed by national,

---

[84]After I finished this essay, David Baddiel (2021) published his angry and funny essay, *Jews Don't Count*, which reflects on the exclusion of Jews from the category of 'minority' and on what he calls 'Schrödinger's White', whereby Jews are attacked both for being non-white, or even destroying whiteness, and for being too white and thus privileged. As James Baldwin wrote about the Jew for his battles, 'the only relevance is that he is white' ([1967] 1969: 10); to be clear, Baldwin also wrote in the same essay, 'all racist positions baffle and appal me'. On Baldwin, an inspiration, and looking back, see Gordon (2015), and now and forward Glaude (2021). See also Brodkin (1998) and Goldstein (2006).

institutional, gendered, historical self-positioning; and by the dynamics of concealment and speaking out prompted by a history of social or cultural exclusion, and a practice of fought for belonging.

This, my response to the question, 'What is a Jewish classicist?' – to lay my cards on the table – is designedly set against the authoritarian and certain practices of the current politics of identity, in the hope for all of us that a more nuanced, conversational and exploratory politics against the forces of prejudice and exclusion can be discovered and nourished.[85]

[85]Thanks, again, to Catherine Conybeare and Helen Morales for conversations – and sanity – during lockdown; and my deep gratitude to those who made this article possible in different ways, from answering questions, to sharing material, to reading the draft, and, especially, giving time for interviews: Glenn Most, Jas Elsner, Alan Bowman, Froma Zeitlin, Tessa Rajak, Seth Schwartz, Jonathan Price, Erich Gruen, Lisa Maurice, Martin Goodman, Tikva Blaukopf-Schein, Miriam Leonard, Talitha Kearey, Sacha Stern, Seth Schein, David Levene, Paula Frederiksen, Hindy Najman, Anna Uhlig, Stephen Greenblatt, Lena Salaymeh, Constanze Güthenke, Barbara Kowalzig, Katie Fleming, Tim Whitmarsh, Patricia Rosenmeyer, Judith Hallett, Jim Porter, Phiroze Vasunia, Peter Garnsey, Dan Tompkins, David Konstan, Amy Richlin, Harriet Fertik, Molly Meyerowitz Levine, Rosa Andujar, Theo Dunkelgrun, Rebecca Laemmle and Michael Silk.

3

Translation and Transformation

In memoriam Neil Hopkinson

i The culture of translation and the translation of culture

Matthew Arnold gives us this illuminating glimpse into his personal life: 'I read five pages of the Greek Anthology every day, looking out the words I do not know; this is what I shall always understand by *education* and it does me good and gives me great pleasure.'[1] This apparently off-hand remark is a poised and knowing self-representation that definitely needs some careful unpacking. It makes a difference, of course, that it is Matthew Arnold who is speaking. He was one of the great gurus of culture for Victorian Britain, whose work on Hellenism and Hebraism linked the two pasts of the Bible and classical antiquity into a provocative matrix of self-understanding.[2] With Arnold, we

---

[1] Arnold (1908: 207).
[2] Collini (1994) and DeLaura (1969).

should be reminded how long and profound the interconnections of the Jewish and the Greek traditions are, back, of course, to Hellenistic Alexandria or the Talmud's distaste for learning Greek, but, for my purposes here, embedded in the specific history of the modern university and its sense of culture and the university's place in it.[3] Arnold – and what Arnold stands for in terms of nineteenth-century cultural values – is fundamental to the history of what I have been discussing in the first two chapters: the modern construction of 'The Jewish Question'. Arnold in his role as public intellectual challenged his readers to recognize their own Philistine lack of truly civilized quality, their failure to live up to the Hellenic ideals of sweetness and light. (He has little interest in *real Jews*: he uses Hebraism as a figure to make his polemic, which, as with John Chrysostom, nonetheless contributes to a discourse whose impact is more painful. His culturally typical dismissiveness towards the actual Jews he spots on the street doesn't help.) Here, however, Arnold is, first of all, telling us, designedly, of his continuing personal engagement with the 'necessity for Greek',[4] on a daily basis – his own habit of cultural betterment.

He was also – more pragmatically – an Inspector of Schools who wrote instrumental reports recommending a broadening of education to include English studies over and against the classical training prevalent in the elite system; he also compared the more developed German system of higher education with the *ad hoc* mess that characterized British universities before the university reform acts.[5] What it meant to know Greek and, in particular, what its place in the educational system should be, was heatedly debated in Victorian politics, because it was well recognized that changing the educational

---

[3]Leonard (2012) for the nineteenth-century intellectual framework here.

[4]Arnold (1960–77: vol. 10: 72), a description of the primeval desire of 'our hairy ancestor', an ironic Darwinian conceit.

[5]Connell (1950) is seminal; Rapple (2017) and Caulfield (2013).

curriculum and its embedded values would change the direction of society – a debate whose heritage we are still struggling with today.[6] Arnold tells us what *he* means by *education* not just because of this ongoing debate, but because he offers this self-portrait as a reader of Greek in one of his reports, which is precisely about educational reform, and he wants to give us a snapshot of his ideals. It is a charged image. The gentleman sits alone and reads Greek. Despite his more radical proposals for a widening of education and a democratizing change of focus away from classics, he himself is part of the elite hierarchy that has profited and will profit from a classical education. This education has two parts: it is formative, in a moral or social sense: it 'does him good' (a typical Victorian educational aim, signally for cold baths and beatings); it is also deeply pleasurable for him – thus fulfilling the paired aims of 'benefit' and 'pleasure' that form a staple of *classical* rhetoric, as he expects his readers to appreciate. The text he specifies – the Greek Anthology – also embeds him in the group of men who translated particular, selected poems from this collection of epigrams and circulated them between each other: a homosocial bonding through shared cultural privilege and performance.[7] Arnold recommends change but displays his position of civilized authority, lightly but firmly declared.

Arnold also admits that he 'looks out' words he does not know (we would say, 'notes and looks up'): it is an exercise in *translation*, not just reading for benefit and pleasure. Translation lay at the heart of classical education in the nineteenth century, and is still central to pretty well every department of classics in the world today. The Victorian classroom was dominated by drilling in grammar and the performance of translation, from school through university – both translation from

---

[6]Discussed at length in Goldhill (2002: 178–245).
[7]Nisbet (2013).

Greek and Latin into English, and, as we will shortly see in detail, from English and other vernacular languages into Greek and Latin.[8] *Tom Brown's Schooldays,* set in Rugby under the headmastership of Matthew's father, Thomas Arnold, is full of scenes of classroom dramas of translating, complete with the moral horror at the possibility of cheating at it. Arnold is representing himself as indulging in an activity that started for him at his father's knee and continues throughout his life. It is part of what has made him who he is. Translation is transformative. If, for Arnold, modern culture must be understood and evaluated as a translation of Hellenic and Hebraic values into modernity, so the performance of translating Greek is an act of personal transformation – *Bildung,* the watchword of the German educationalists he so admired: an education into civilized values. Arnold – therefore – also wrote the most influential and provocative contemporary study of literary translation, which concentrated on Homer and how Homer could and should be rendered into English for modern culture.[9] For Arnold, translation links the detailed work of educational practice and reform, to personal development, to aesthetics, to social change. His self-description with which I started may look casual, but it is knowing and pointed. He is a maven of *translation.*

Arnold's sense of the importance of translation is instructive. All of us classicists *do* translation. Learning Greek and Latin and translating its texts into English (or whichever language is your own) is the usual beginning of a serious classical training – often primed by courses in myth or literature – *in translation,* as we constantly remind each other. But because translation is such meat and drink to the profession, its broader implications are often left underexplored, or allowed to be discussed under the aegis of translation studies, which has made great

---

[8]Stray (1998) and Stray, ed. (1999) are the best introductions.
[9]Arnold (1861).

strides in appreciating the linguistics of moving between languages, but has less commonly engaged in the long *cultural* history of translation as a process of transformation.[10] It should be impossible, indeed, to tell the story of classics and classicism without recognizing the *disruptive necessity* of translation. My highlights of such a history would certainly include, from the outset, how Roman engagement with Greek culture was a cultural battle of translation – of genres, values, self-understanding. There would be no Latin literature without translation.[11] Virgil tells the story of Rome's foundation through his appropriations of Greek epic – just as Roman comedy redrafts Greek scripts. Roman writers revert repeatedly to their compulsive, ambivalent, loving, dismissive, needy engagements with Hellenism's cultural prestige. My highlights would also include the history of the place of the Bible in the West as a history of conflict over translation, whether we look (as we shortly will) at the Septuagint's Greek version of the Hebrew text, or Jerome's authorized Latin version of the Greek Testament – or, most pertinently and violently, Erasmus' retranslation of the Latin text from the newly recovered Greek sources – a process which fuelled the violence and social upheavals of the Reformation.[12] The language of English literature, in turn, is richly veined with the language of the King James Bible – which is a translation replete with the Protestant ideology of the era of its production.[13] What's more, translating the Bible into the languages of communities about to feel the force of Western imperial power was an integral element of the British Empire, which marched with a gun in one hand and Scripture

---

[10] Introductions to translation theory include: Steiner (1975), Gentzler (1993), Venuti (1995), Bassnett (2002) and Pym (2014). Seminal discussion of Latin/Greek bilingualism is Adams (2003), extended by Elder and Mullen (2019).

[11] See Goldhill (forthcoming b) and the provocative Feeney (2016).

[12] Rajak (2009) and Goldhill (2002).

[13] See Tadmor (2010), with the background of Sheehan (2005) and Shuger (1994).

in the other.[14] Translation is a theological requirement (no one now is a native speaker of ancient Greek or ancient Hebrew), but also an instrument of imperialism: *translatio imperii* and *translatio scientiae* go hand in hand. At the broadest level, any engagement with antiquity requires such a practice of translation to make antiquity comprehensible to modernity. It is, to adapt what Horace said of Greek for Romans, how we get the past and the past gets us. The history of classicism – each era's sequential and ongoing relation to its image of the past of Greece and Rome – is best seen as not so much changes in 'taste', as *re-translations*, re-figurations of how people form their expressivity and self-understanding through an engagement with the other of antiquity. Each generation needs its own translations.

At another level, the study of classics has always promised to transform you. The gatekeepers of the discipline insist that as a philologist, a lover of ancient languages, you will, like Bottom, the ludicrous lover of Shakespeare's *Midsummer Night's Dream*, be 'translated'. All education has a claim to be transformative, but classics has often striven – sometimes with confidence, sometimes with a certain desperation – to demonstrate the formative value of its nuts-and-bolts work of learning Greek and Latin grammar and turning the texts of the past into serviceable English (or whatever language is pertinent). Classics – the business of translation – teaches how to structure thought; it teaches order and regularity; it teaches discipline – all these and many other claims are prevalent in the field's self-justifications over the last couple of centuries. Such claims, under pressure from educational reformists, could become foolishly overexaggerated. For J. K. Stephen, Virginia Woolf's cousin, so strong is the formative power of Greek that *'having known Greek'* is enough: learn it once and then totally forget it, and you will still be the better

---

[14]Porter (2004) and Stanley (1990).

person for it . . .[15] (Stephen, mind you, loved his own performative outrageousness: he was an unpleasantly snobby and outspoken misogynist, who was thought by some, unconvincingly, to be Jack the Ripper; his psychological demons ultimately led him to starve himself to death, which would probably today be classed as a rare case of anorexia in a middle-aged man). Yet, for all the wilder claims made on behalf of learning how to translate Greek and Latin, it is still the case that it *does* become part of every classicist's self-recognition: we all have a story of translation. By which, I mean more than a memory of those exams, or a tale of a ludicrous student error: we are transformed by our professional training and career as we practice translating. To tell the history of translation as part of the discipline is not just a history of an integral technique of classics, but also the narrative of the personal formation of classicists.

The painter G. F. Watts captures some of what I am talking about in a wonderful painting of 1868, that is co-temporaneous with Arnold's *Culture and Anarchy*, and was discussed with fascination by the poet Algernon Swinburne when it was exhibited that year.[16] The picture is entitled, *The Wife of Pygmalion. A translation from the Greek*. It depicts a beautiful woman, from the waist up, with one of her breasts bared. She looks halfaway from the viewer's gaze, strikingly unemotional, stiff and still – like a statue – but with a soft fleshliness and colour that the light falling across her breasts emphasizes. (Swinburne, of course, was the leading light of the poets despised by the conservatives as the 'fleshly school of poetry': not Arnold's Hellenism, not at all.)[17] The picture was modelled on a bust in the Arundel Marbles collection, Watts tells us, a statue that Watts suggested was a masterpiece worthy

---

[15]Stephen (1891: 13).
[16]Swinburne (1925–7: 197); on which, see Evangelista (2010, especially 169–70).
[17]See Prins (1999: 112–73).

of Pheidias.[18] Watts depicts in paint a woman who was a statue and has come to life, an image based on a statue found broken in pieces in a cellar and restored to splendour. The story of Pygmalion and his statue wife has become a material object, a painting of a sculpture. It is a Greek story – but we have only Latin versions of it (most famously, Ovid's). It is not 'rather misleading'[19] that Watts calls it a 'translation from the Greek', but a pithy and witty recognition that his painting is a 'translation' of a statue that represents the story of a statue that is 'translated' into a woman, which is a story already a 'translation' from Greek myth into Latin and now into Victorian England. Between Greek and Latin, between Greek, Latin and English, between media, she is translated . . .

There is one further narrative cued by my opening story of Arnold. For Arnold and his readers, the opposition of Hellenism and Hebraism worked persuasively not simply because of the long history of opposition between Jewish and Greek traditions, but also because of the recognition of the importance of Hebrew for understanding Christianity and its sacred texts that resulted in the growing institutionalization of these twin roots of European culture in European learning. *The* classical languages were understood again (as they had been in the early modern era of Erasmus) as Latin, Greek and Hebrew.[20] Each privileged ancient language – Arabic, in particular – was declared to have had a classical phase. Although classics as a discipline in recent years has often prided itself on 'opening up' the discipline to new intellectual currents , a claim which often goes hand in hand with dismissing the narrowness of the nineteenth-century curriculum – an understandable reaction to that

---

[18]Watts (1913: 237–8, discussed by Ribeyrol 2018: 181–2).
[19]Ribeyrol (2018: 180).
[20]For early modern, see Grafton and Weinberg (2011); in general, see Wiese and Thulin, eds (2021).

curriculum if nothing else – nonetheless, the linguistic narrowing of the field is also a striking feature of our modernity. Few modern classicists would be comfortable with biblical Hebrew, just as few read the Septuagint in their Hellenistic courses. With Arnold's commitment to Hellenism and Hebraism as a framework for understanding *modern* culture, we can also see how our modern disciplinary culture has, in turn, restricted and delimited the Mediterranean's linguistic richness into two languages, and not even the full range of those. To be a Jewish classicist is to inhabit a field which has systematically removed ancient Hebrew from its shelves.

This final chapter therefore follows three strands of enquiry, which together offer a different style of history of the discipline from the personal narrative of Chapter 1 and the socio-anthropology of Chapter 2: here we look at how the infrastructure of the field's work gets organized, its effect on the scholar and how this alters an engagement with the past. I start with an account of a prime moment in the history of the practice of translation, when it was, indeed, central to the educational system at schools and universities, especially in Britain: the Victorian obsession with verse and prose composition. This history has not yet been told, but it is, I think, revelatory and riveting, especially when framed against Walter Benjamin's analysis of translation, which has become so influential in modern criticism. (Walter Benjamin, I probably do not need to emphasize, was a Jewish scholar whose suicide was in direct response to his desperate plight under the Nazis, and who could have been included in the roll call of Jewish scholars in Chapter 2.) This discussion of composition in Latin and Greek, in contrast to the usual scope of translation studies, even when following Benjamin's sophisticated prompts, is focused on how translation, in this case at least, is not aimed at making available texts written in otherwise incomprehensible languages to an otherwise excluded audience, but rather an exercise of transformation where *both* languages are known and appreciated by the imagined reader as well as the translator – that is, where translation shuttles *between* languages and cultures in a display of recognized difference and appropriation, a display of skill to the knowing.

Second, however, I trace how this privileged, educational task of translation becomes explicitly recognized as an activity of self-formation and plays a role in the bonding of the elite of Victorian culture – and how this past has been received today (not least in my own education). The lifelong practice of translation is a technology of self-advancement within a competitive scholarly world, a performance of a scholarly way of inhabiting a literary world – and thus related back to the first chapter's thoughts on how the personal is narrated in and relevant to a person's scholarship. Third, this discussion of self-formation opens into a consideration of how *tradition* in the discipline of classics is to be understood, analysed, criticized today – and what it means for a classicist now to take up a position 'within the tradition of the discipline'. There is no more 'traditional' exercise than translating: to translate is always also to set yourself in a line of translators and translations. Translation thus leads back to the opening question of the book: how a personal stance within classics as a discipline and as a history is narrated and acknowledged.

It is integral to the agenda of this book that a subject as apparently technical as translating turns out to be so closely intertwined with both personal and political narratives – although it is regularly disavowed as such in today's academy, even when it is fully recognized as having such implications in earlier eras. Nobody today, nobody at least in any classics department, is likely to be burned to death for a translation error – as is gruesomely attested in the religious conflicts of the Reformation. Yet, when Emily Wilson announces she is the first (English-speaking) woman to have published a translation of the *Odyssey*, she is claiming to re-vision the *Odyssey* through female eyes, a claim that would take a great deal of analysis at a political and personal level to explore fully (not least in relation to the novels of Madelaine Miller, Pat Barker, Margaret Atwood or Natalie Haynes).[21] Or when Sarah Ruden offers her new translation of the Gospels, promising to cut away generations of theological accretion – so that 'Behold the Man!' becomes 'Look at this guy!' – we can see how strong an agenda – personal and political – underlies her project, which is explicitly and necessarily highly self-conscious of the long list of translations of scripture it is adding to.[22] I started this chapter with Matthew Arnold not just because he is so influential in imagining how the tradition of the Hebrew Bible and Greek classicism interrelate (one theme of this book), but also, as pressingly, because he makes it abundantly clear that translation is a matter of transformation between cultures and in culture, a transformation both of texts and of readers and writers. This chapter's quarry is to see what is at stake for any of us when we translate and see our work within a line – a tradition – of translations. What does it take to transform you into a classicist and what is it to transform your culture through classicism? And for a Jewish classicist . . .?

ii Walter Benjamin meets Henry Montagu Butler

Walter Benjamin begins his seminal essay on translation with a bold statement that strikes at the heart of any theory or practice of reception studies. 'When seeking knowledge of a work of art or an art form, it never proves useful to take the receiver into account.'[23] For Benjamin,

---

[21]Wilson (2017), Miller (2011, 2018), Barker (2018), Atwood (2005) and Haynes (2019).
[22]Ruden (2021).
[23]Benjamin (1997: 151).

it would seem, the art work exists in and for itself, an inheritance of his conflicted intellectual roots in German idealist philosophy. No *Rezeptionsgeschichte* here: 'Not only is every effort to relate art to a specific public or its representatives misleading,' he continues, 'but the very concept of an "ideal" receiver is spurious' (1971: 151). It could generously be allowed that the multiplicity of audiences, the complex dynamics of misunderstanding and contingency that an audience's engagement also involve, and the evident ideologically charged and self-interested projection of art's 'ideal' audience, are likely, indeed, to make all too many declarations of what an audience must see or comprehend, seem crassly oversimplified critical assumptions. But Benjamin more challengingly goes on: 'no work of art presupposes [human] attention. No poem is meant for the reader, no picture for the beholder, no symphony for the audience' (1971: 151).

This opening paragraph is foundational for his influential discussion of translation that follows. Benjamin discusses translation at a theoretical level that largely avoids any historically framed examples; but he also focuses almost entirely on the *production* of translation, on how the foreignness of languages to each other is the necessary condition of the impossibility of fulfilled translation. He writes simply and beautifully of how connotations – his example is *brot* in German and *pain* in French – are not transferable between words in other languages. He seeks to escape from his melancholy sense of alienation and loss by imagining a sort of translation that seeks to go beyond the foreignness of languages to reach towards a greater or pure language of art, a domain where 'languages are reconciled and fulfilled' (1971: 158). Translation, he argues, 'must lovingly, and in detail, fashion in its own language a counterpart to the original's mode of intention, in order to make both of them recognizable as fragments of a vessel, as fragments of a greater language' (1971: 161). It is not by chance that on the same page Benjamin quotes the opening verse of the Gospel of

John, and, indeed, concludes his essay with the surprising claim that: 'The interlinear version of the holy scriptures is the prototype or ideal of all translation' (1971: 165). The paraphrase or translation of scripture is an ideal because it presupposes, in Benjamin's view, that revealed scripture, the sacred text, is constituted precisely as the sought-after language, where meaning so far transcends the mere materiality of expression that translation can proceed without loss, without deficit. Benjamin's melancholy comes not so much from the simple failure of one language to capture the connotations of another but from the inevitable inability of language to fulfil its own potential of translatability. Benjamin's conclusion underlines the spiritual longing that runs through the essay and which has attracted so many of his readers.

It would not be hard to show that the idealism with which Benjamin invests such an 'interlinear version of the holy scriptures' bears a very precarious relation to the history of translating the Bible.[24] On the one hand, he is, of course, correct that from the Letter of Aristeas,[25] or, with a more developed if quite unconvincing theoretical apparatus, from Philo, we have the story of the Septuagint, the Greek translation of the Bible, being composed of seventy-two experts in separate rooms, all of whom produce the same version. The languages of Greek and Hebrew, claims Philo, are like sisters running together.[26] There is no gap between the languages, no gap between words and things. The business of translating the Septuagint was like a mathematical process of exchanging agreed symbols: 'as in geometry or logic, I think, where signs do not allow the variation of interpretation, but remain unchanged in their set, original form, so in this same way the translators found the words to correspond to things, the sole or best expression

---

[24]Bentley (1983), François (2016), Gelhaus (1989), MacDonald (2016), Pelikan (1996), Sheehan (2005) and Shuger (1994).
[25]Gruen (2008), Honigman (2007) and Pearce (2007).
[26]*Mos* 2. 37.

for what was to be revealed'.[27] Philo's assertion of translation without
loss is wholly in service of his cultural vision of hybridity, where Greek
and Jewish traditions combine in mutual fulfilment, an image he
embodies in his own self-representation.[28] For Philo, Reuben, Joseph's
brother, can quote Plato.[29] The frankly ludicrous claim that Hebrew
and Greek are so alike that translation is like swapping mathematical
symbols is a sign of Philo's deep ideological commitment to such
cultural hybridity.

Augustine, on the other hand, already demonstrates a more
profoundly expressed awareness of how insufficient the materiality of
human words is to God's language; he determines that the true version
of God's language can only be heard internally, in silence.[30] (For
Benjamin, the 'monstrous and original danger of all translation' is that
the very openness of language might 'lock up the translator in silence'
[1971: 164].) For Augustine, human words are a barrier as much as a
route towards comprehension. 'If you have understood something, it is
not God,' he sums up this apophatic theology.[31] As the Christian
centuries unfurl, there is a far more contested and bitter story. In late
antiquity, the Septuagint and the Gospels were re-translated into better,
more intellectual Greek for a more self-consciously elite Greek-speaking
Christian community: the simplicity of the Gospels was insufficient to
the aesthetic ambitions and theological dictates of a sophisticated and
educated elect.[32] In the battles of the Reformation, men were put to death
for translating the Bible into vernacular languages; the Reformation
itself was fuelled by new and shocking translations of the Greek of the

---

[27] *Mos* 2. 38–9.
[28] Niehoff (2001, 2018).
[29] *De Jos* 1.17.
[30] See Ando (1990) and Harrison (2000).
[31] *Serm*. 117.
[32] Goldhill (forthcoming a), with extended bibliography.

Gospels – for which Erasmus became an unwilling icon.[33] If the King James Bible is the archetype of how translation can produce a new national language, it had a bloody and violent birthing in the previous century.[34] In the nineteenth century, the thousands of translations of the Bible, now collected in the British and Foreign Bible Society archive, were agents of missionary and imperialist activity, where, as we have already noted, the Bible, gun or flag were equally likely to be waved.[35] To choose Holy Scripture as his example of ideal translation requires from Benjamin a *theological* comprehension of its language, which represses the violent contingencies and consequences of biblical controversy and imperialism. The lack of any *politics of translation* in Benjamin's essay is marked: in his story, nobody is murdered for their translation. Benjamin's initial refusal to countenance 'the receiver' of translation excludes from his narrative both the policemen of translation who killed for the authority of the Church, and the subjects of empire who experienced the Bible as a weapon of domination. Benjamin's argument, even when it broaches the pragmatics of translating, floats free of cultural history.

This chapter, however, is initially concerned with two other aspects of Benjamin's resistance to 'the receiver' or 'the reader' as an integral aspect of translation. First, I want to consider how translation can indeed be an object as well as a process of exchange, and can play a role in social formation precisely through such interactive dynamics. Making and sharing translations can be an instrumental vector in the formation of networks and the exercise of self-formation – the praxis of *Bildung*. Translations can be written precisely with a 'receiver' in mind, for the attention of a reader. How does translation help make you who you are? Second, I want to consider the interrelated question of how reading an original and a translation *together* changes what this performance of

---

[33]Goldhill (2002: 14–59) and Jardine (1993).
[34]See Tadmor (2010), with the background of Sheehan (2005) and Shuger (1994).
[35]Porter (2004) and Stanley (1990).

translation can mean. In particular, I will be looking at the expectations of bilingual reading, of what it means to read *between* languages. Benjamin is aware, of course, that a translator – of all figures – must move between languages, and writes in striking terms about how a 'home language' can be mobilized or transformed by its encounter with another language. What translatability means for the force of language is a central plank of his argument. But his interest is first in the completed translation and its trajectory towards either the transcendence of the 'greater language' or, as he ends, the fulfilment of a sacred text: for him, as for Philo, translation aims ideally at a single voice. I will be exploring rather how the dynamic space between languages is inhabited, when reading is also self-consciously and productively shuttling between and across different languages.

My test case for this discussion will be the practice of translating poetry from English (and other modern languages) into Greek and Latin in the later Victorian and Edwardian era in Britain. This focus may sound recondite or parochial. It should not. The British Empire was the dominant political force in the world throughout the nineteenth and early twentieth centuries, whose impact on the political order is still being experienced. The administrators and officials of this imperial project were trained in the public schools and universities of the country. Classics formed a significantly large portion of the curriculum, as has been extensively analysed of late, and within this curriculum 'composing' played a strikingly important role.[36] As Gildersleeve in America snorted, 'Classical education in England has been, for long years, one huge polyp of verse-making' (this, part of Gildersleeve's youthful pro-German anti-Englishness).[37] The best classicists were marked out by their ability in

---

[36]Following the seminal Stray (1998) and Stray, ed. (1999).
[37]Gildersleeve (1992: 13). See Briggs (2002).

writing Greek and Latin, and especially verse. This institutionalization and privileging of composition was a uniquely British practice. In the rest of Europe, including the philological hothouse of Germany, composition remained a minority concern.[38] In Britain, however, it pervaded education: more than fifty textbooks on how to write such verse were published. For those who went on to university, it was an expected training. *Aufgabe*, 'exercise', 'task', with a subtext of 'duty', is a key critical term for Benjamin's analysis of translation. Within the elite world of highly educated men in nineteenth-century Britain, translation between Greek, Latin and English – both from the classical languages into English and from English into the classical languages – was the *Aufgabe par excellence*, a privileged educational practice that continued into the milieu of cultural performance. Moving between the private and public realms, between schooldays and adult leisure, between remembered past and proclaimed expertise, translation ran through the life of British men as a thread of self-conscious civilized attainment.

The translation exercises that created the hierarchies of remembered success and failure at school, became a form of bonding between men, not least in the heightened male environments of university, the law, the army, empire. Gideon Nisbet, for example, has insightfully traced how men translated Greek epigrams, often of a carefully erotic nature, and circulated them first in letters and then in small often privately published volumes, thus creating a select homosocial community of literary self-expression.[39] William Cory, to take an exemplary case, was a flamboyant teacher at Eton, who revelled in intense relationships with some of the boys in his charge, his 'favourites'.[40] (His is a story that would result in

---

[38]On German philological cathexis and its networking, see Güthenke (2020).
[39]Nisbet (2013).
[40]Brett (1923), Compton Mackenzie (1950) and Goldhill (2016b: 94–6, 152–3). Cory wrote a guide to writing Latin lyric verse (1871), at the time something of a rarity, and a guide to Greek Iambics (1873). Carter (1949) gives the history of publication.

prosecution today.) He was indiscrete in such affections and was forced
to leave teaching, though he left behind a cult of romantic friendship
among boys that continued to vex the school authorities (he went to live
in Hampstead in London where he became a private tutor, and, to his
and everyone else's surprise, late in life fell in love with a young woman,
married and had a child.) He remained well connected and well loved by
his fellow teachers and former pupils, many of whom became major
public figures. His biographical reminiscences and his poetry were avidly
read by the next generation of single men, searching for a language of
desire and the self. He published a slim volume of English verses called
Ionica, a title that screams its roots in Greek desire. Its most famous
poem is a translation of an epigram by Callimachus, which begins, 'They
told me, Heraclitus, they told me you were dead ...' Callimachus wrote,
'εἶπε τις Ἡράκλειτε τέον μόρον,' which we might translate with lumpy
literalness, 'Someone told me, Heraclitus, your fate ...' Cory's brilliant
rendition, 'They told me, Heraclitus, they told me you were dead,' is made
so powerfully moving by the repetition of 'they told me', and becomes
particularly effective and affecting against the single and simple *eipe tis*,
'someone told'. The echoing 'they told me, they told me', recalls how many
times this poem has been translated and re-versioned. There is a self-
reflexivity of literary reproduction in the repetition of 'they told me', an
echo of the tradition of echoes that is the classical tradition. It also signals
the very circulation of chat about friends that the circulation of the
poem performed. So, paradigmatically, John Addington Symonds,
struggling with his sexuality, was given a copy of *Ionica*, by his tutor at
Oxford, John Conington, who mentored him through a crisis of sexual
tale-telling that led to the headmaster of Harrow, Vaughan, having his
career thwarted by the threat of exposure for his sexual advances to a
friend of Symonds.[41] 'They told me, they told of me, they told on me ...'

---

[41]Goldhill (2016b: 98–9) for the story; on Symonds, see Nisbet (2013), Kaplan (2005),
Pemble, ed. (2000) and Brady (2005: 157–209).

Henry Montagu Butler, who became headmaster at Harrow after Vaughan, and eventually the Master of Trinity College, Cambridge, moved in an adjacent and a more illustrious circle. He privately sent his Greek hexameter translation of the biblical story of David and Goliath to various grandees.[42] The classicists Kennedy and Butcher, both famous translators in their own right, wrote back in admiration; Prime Minister Gladstone, who in 1861 had published a collection of his translations together with Edward Lyttelton (future headmaster of Eton and international sports hero),[43] invited him to breakfast. John Addington Symonds – a linking mediator between the two groups of men – wrote: 'The Homeric rendering of the David and Goliath episode seems to my taste perfect. Unlike the armour of Saul upon David, the Greek of the *Iliad* fits the Bible narrative without cumbrousness of any kind' – as if, in Philo's terms, the poetic forms of the *Iliad* and biblical narrative were sisters, at home together. Gladstone would have delighted in such a judgment, as indicated by his pamphlet proving the parallel providential narratives of Homer and the Hebrew Bible (we'll come back to this pamphlet).[44] Erich Auerbach, a good friend of Walter Benjamin, in the celebrated first chapter of *Mimesis*, argues that Homeric narrative and biblical narrative are opposed and irreconcilable modes of representation. Not so for Montagu Butler and his readers, for whom translation between such modes is integral to their engagement with the multiple pasts of antiquity. Matthew Arnold, whose matrix of Hebraism and Hellenism, as we have already said, defined the genealogies of cultural

---

[42]Graham (1920: 372–4).

[43]Lyttelton and Gladstone (1861, 2nd edn 1863). Lyttelton, who was Headmaster of Eton, 1905–16, scored a century for Middlesex against the Australians, and played football once for England against Scotland. Lyttelton (1897), a defence of verse composition, indicates an early fear of its decline.

[44]Gange (2009).

self-definition for later Victorians, was an outlier in thinking Montagu Butler's version 'a rather strange tour de force'. Such poems circulated first between friends; they might be published in a journal; they might end up in a volume. The circulation and dissemination of such translations defined a network of friends; the private circle became public as anecdotes and finally publication allowed a portal for others. The image of friends writing to each other, and the lasting worth of such poems over death is the very subject of Cory's, 'They told me, Heraclitus . . .', a theme which Cory's translation enacts in full. The performance of translation is the means and matter of male social bonding: translation and its gift forms the *translatio amicitiae*.

At another level, major intellectual debates flared around the proper translation of Homer, led by Matthew Arnold's celebrated and much criticized Oxford lectures on the subject: hence the poignancy of *his* comment to Montagu Butler on his Iliadic account of David and Goliath.[45] Fired not least by the contemporary discoveries of Schliemann, the question of what constituted the proper modern translational style for ancient Homer was an insistent issue of cultural genealogy – how the past could enter the present, how the present formed its relation to the past – in a way that went far beyond aesthetics into the realm of cultural values. Translation was not just an intellectual flashpoint, but also a commercial business, led by companies such as Bohn's, providing both cribs for schoolboys, and a higher level of literary production for an aspirational readership.[46] Although Erasmus' and More's translations of Lucian in early modern Europe were a financial as well as critical success, and Pope's *Iliad* likewise in the eighteenth century, it is only as the nineteenth century progresses that translation becomes a major international industry whose impact is felt at multiple levels of the now

---

[45]Arnold (1861). He was even criticized for not lecturing in Latin.
[46]Stray (2018).

vastly increased reading public. For men like Montagu Butler, the issue of translation, in the right voice, as a basis of a proper education, and the consequent relation of contemporary ideals to the tradition of antiquity, required a lifelong engagement: a cultural genealogy. 'I can scarcely remember the time when I did not make, love and soon after do my best to teach Latin and Greek verses,' he recalled.[47] 'The old habit of composing has clung to me as a perfect companion,' he wrote in retrospective melancholy, just before the First World War.[48] The act of composing is like the imagined friend who is to read it, the perfect companion, the ideal reader.

The journal, *Classical Review* (*CR*), opens a revelatory vista onto a section of this activity. The journal was first published at the height of the educational and cultural status of verse composition, and through this one publication we can see in a focused way both how pervasive and valued composition had become, and the history of its gradual decline. Founded in 1887 (and still going strong), *Classical Review* began with a mixed portfolio of research articles, mainly of a philological tenor, reviews of books, archaeological reports, obituaries, surveys of other journals, letters on topics of debate, and, from its first edition, translations of English, Italian and German poetry into Greek and Latin.[49] In 1894, the journal tidied its contributions into titled sections: 'original contributions', 'reviews', 'notes', 'archaeology', and a business section of correspondence and summaries of other journals.

'Versions' immediately started appearing in the review section, and almost every edition of *Classical Review*, including the years of the First World War, printed at least one usually Greek verse translation of a modern poem. Several editions have as many as four lengthy poems

---

[47]Montagu Butler (1913: 5).
[48]Montagu Butler (2014: x).
[49]On the foundation of *CR*, see Stray (2018).

in Greek or Latin. In the 1920s, the habit shrinks to only brief, witty epigrams (anyone now who turned to a piece immediately after the Russian Revolution entitled 'Bolshevism', might expect more than an elegantly dismissive Greek couplet, the contribution of the 1919 volume of *CR* to world events),[50] and gradually through the 1930s even this form of publication trickles into silence, lamented in 1943 as the unreplaced loss of a generation of giants: 'Montagu Butler, Archer Hind, Verrall, Walter Headlam are dead, and the death of the last of them brought an era to a close.'[51] As late as 1977, however, a review of a book of compositions was written by Ted Kenney in Latin elegiacs.[52] In 1897, in an unparalleled section of its own, entitled, for the first time, 'Translations', a single poem appeared (with notes): a 200-line rendition of Leopardi's ode on Dante's grave written in Pindaric stanzas by Sir Richard Jebb, the greatest of Montagu Butler's pupils in composition.[53] In the inevitably competitive world of men writing verses to show off their facility in ancient languages and poetic skill, 200 lines of Pindaric complexity (from the Italian . . .) was the nuclear option. But it should also be noted that Leopardi, whose own poetry turned again and again to Romantic Hellenism, was reflecting on his own place in the great tradition of Italian poetry, as Jebb takes Leopardi's lyricism and transforms it into a mirror of the founding figure of grand Romantic lyric, Pindar. Jebb's translation is a layered act of cultural genealogy. It mediates between the Greek tradition and the Italian tradition in the name of a shared European poetic landscape. In the 1890s, classicism remained a shared language.

In this grandest of compositional modes, *Classical Review* also published a 154-line 'Greek ode on the eighth centenary of the

---

[50]*CR*, 33 (1919: 165).
[51]*CR*, 57 (1943: 1, Harrison, E. 'Latin Verse Composition and the Nasonian Code').
[52]Kenney (1977).
[53]*CR*, 12 (1897: 369–75).

University of Bologna', also by Jebb, of course;[54] a further ode in a bizarre metrical scheme – it puts together different ancient metres in an unparalleled (and centauric) combination – for the 200th anniversary of the foundation of Yale, by Thomas Dwight Goodell of Yale, who published the music itself elsewhere;[55] and a long lyric translation of verses from the Wisdom of Solomon by Walter Headlam, another of the greats whose loss was lamented in 1943.[56] But translating verses was also the practice of the gentleman at leisure, and this social medium privileged cleverness, wit and bonhomie. So, the first edition included a Greek translation of John Gay's theatrical ballad 'Black-eyed Susan' by George Denman.[57] Denman was a High Court Judge and, finally, Privy Counsellor, who had also sat as a Member of Parliament for the Liberal Party. He had already translated into Latin Gray's 'Elegy', and, more bizarrely, Pope's *Iliad* – and dedicated it to his friend, Prime Minister Gladstone, whose classical interests were fundamental to his political sense of world history. For the insider readers of *Classical Review*, a particular pleasure here is seeing one of the very grandest of British public figures, translating such a trivial sentimental song into a classicizing form through the school-learned and still continued language of verse composition.

So, maximizing the disjunction between the technical skills of writing in an ancient language and metre, and the humbleness of folk poetry, in 1893 *Classical Review* published R. Y. Tyrrell's version of 'Scots wha hae' in Sapphics;[58] and, in a self-consciously 'new departure in the art of Greek verse writing', Tyrrell (again) turned Captain Morris' raucous drinking song, 'A Toper's Apology', into the form of a

---

[54]*CR*, 2 (1888: 257–0).

[55]*CR*, 16 (1902: 67–8).

[56]*CR*, 17 (1903: 229–31). On Headlam, see Goldhill (2002: 232–43).

[57]*CR*, 1 (1887: 76).

[58]*CR*, 7 (1893: 279–80).

(very long) Greek skolion in the style of the familiar Athenian little song for the symposium about the tyrannicides, Aristogeiton and Harmodius.[59] Tyrrell also translated 'Three Jolly Post Boys' into a non-classical metre, a license, which the editors who published the poem, promised would *not* be indulged again.[60] John Sargeaunt, head of classics at Westminster and famous for his – and the school's – skills at composition upped the ante by a bravado Latin translation of Browning's 'Soliloquy of the Spanish Cloister'. Browning , a poetic celebrity, was a common choice for such compositions, but this poem was crazily unsuitable, with abstruse vocabulary – 'cork-crop' 'oak-galls' – culminating in the rhetorical question, which seemed particularly to challenge the school-master, 'What's the Greek name for Swine-snout?' He headed his remarkable version, *in piam memoriam sonitus verborum iam paene obsoleti,* 'in pious memory of the sound of words now almost lost'.[61] *In piam memoriam* is a phrase also to open a toast: you can almost hear Sargeaunt raising his glass to his achievement. These drinking songs and other games in smart verse allowed the writers and readers to see themselves as if they were like Catullus and his pals, at a classical party, showing off.

This sense of a coterie was made into a longing glance into the literary salon. Lewis Campbell wrote a brief letter to the editors, accompanying half a dozen lines of Greek: 'Dear Sir, the enclosed lines, addressed to Mr Robert Browning, and accompanying a little volume of Greek verse, were very graciously received by him last summer, and may on that account have some interest for your readers at the present time.'[62] Browning was *the* literary superstar of the immediately preceding decades, a lion to be lionized, who had died

[59]*CR*, 7 (1893: 368-9).
[60]*CR*, 19 (1905: 73–4).
[61]*CR*, 20 (1906: 414–15).
[62]*CR*, 4 (1890: 61).

the year before. The apparent mixture of self-promotion and celebrity-hunting is not usual for Campbell, sensitive, unassuming, serious Scottish Christian and friend of Jowett:[63] talking about one's own verse composition, however, seemed to bring out the boyish competition in those who had learned it hard at school. And, for the readers of the journal, the exchange of Greek verses opens a portal into the glamorous imagined world of the Olympians of poetry. This was poetry announced precisely to be written for the attention of its audience, a poem meant for a reader – and we are invited to overhear – to read over the shoulder of – the speaking gift.

The range of thinking and practice about translation was varied and interrelated, however. In the same volume in which Campbell published his letter, there was a 'Greek version of some lines of Coleridge' by the Cambridge don W. T. Lendrum;[64] also, 'Four Versions of Tennyson's "Crossing the Bar"', two in Latin, two in Greek, by E. D. Stone, (one-time Fellow of King's College, Cambridge, and school teacher at Eton), Lewis Campbell, Herbert Kynaston (High Master of St Paul's School, London, whose biography was written by E. D. Stone) and H. M. B. (Henry Montagu Butler, whose last line has an error, I can't resist pointing out, as *ignotus* is surely a misprint for *ignotas*).[65] The four men make a clique; the four versions a shared contest. The competition here is of grandees' 'fair copies'. Each teacher had his own collection of versions to give to pupils. In other contexts, the term 'fair copy' indicates a 'neat' version for formal use, something drafted, corrected and rewritten. But, in the context of compositional exercises, it means a teacher's paradigm for the pupil to imitate. A teacher would collect his own students' best work in a volume often called *Flosculus*, a private memorial of achievement. So, Montagu Butler's biographer recalled that:

---

[63]On Campbell, see Goldhill (2016a).

[64]*CR*, 4 (1890: 131).

[65]*CR*, 4 (1890: 184). The error is silently corrected in Montagu Butler (1914: 312).

'Sent up' copies that reached a standard of almost flawless excellence might win the supreme honour of inscription in 'the Book.' Successful prize exercises, if of sufficient merit, were immortalised in the pink 'Prolusiones' printed for Speech Day, when they were read aloud. 'The Prolusiones and the Book,' [Montagu Butler] wrote in 1910, 'are, I am convinced, the two material engines for keeping up a high standard of scholarship at Harrow.'[66]

Scholarship, we might note, is here co-extensive with its demonstration in this one exercise.

Competition and paraded excellence were integral to the practice of composition (no surprise in the agonistic, game-dominated world of public school education and its continuation into the sports and examinations of university, the trials of the courtroom, the military exploits of the army). Montagu Butler was said to have an extraordinary comprehensive recall for every 'fast horse' that won a composition prize in the system. (It is amusing to see that in a high-profile sermon on Henry Martyn, whose modern martyrdom was commemorated in Truro Cathedral, he could not help mentioning that Martyn had won a prize for verse composition at school, a particular slant on what should go into a hagiography.)[67] Acknowledged or would-be masters of composition published their own versions of translations in volumes which were also earnestly reviewed – and marked for corrections, as if in class.[68] So, C. H. Russell's compositions – Russell taught at Clifton in

---

[66]Graham (1920: 372). Cambridge had earlier published *Prolusiones*, on which the Harrow volumes were presumably modelled.

[67]Montagu Butler (1887: 3). For Martyn's memorial at Truro, see Goldhill (2015: 186–95).

[68]In 1890, two huge volumes of such 'fair copies' were published, the fourth edition of *Sabrinae Corolla* in London (first edition 1850), with a large number of pieces by Kennedy, and *Dublin Greek and Latin Verses* edited by R. Y. Tyrrell in Dublin – together around 1,000 pages and getting towards 100 authors. (Schools and universities competed through such collections of versions from the 1840s onwards. See Tyrrell (1899) for a hagiographic

Bristol, but was otherwise not well known as a scholar – were given an excellent review *and* a string of corrections in this same volume of *Classical Review*.[69]

At greater length, however, William Everett reviewed Way's English verse translation of Homer. William Everett was the son of Edward Everett, the American Secretary of State, who spoke at Gettysburg before Lincoln's famous address, and was himself a member of Congress. He had graduated from Harvard and from Trinity College, Cambridge, which probably explains the commission of the review. Everett notes that it is twenty-nine years since Arnold's lectures on Homer; and reflects that at least seven full-scale verse translations have been published in English since, none of which took due account of Arnold's strictures. Most tellingly, he insists that none of them will have the effect that Pope's version had on his father and grandfather. 'In the first quarter of this century, a New Englander's farmer's book shelf, which was crammed if it had fifty volumes, was sure to have Pope's Homer.'[70] Nowadays, he declares, critics and readers scoff at Pope, but we are still waiting for '*the* translator' who might fulfil such a formative role for a new generation. Everett, in reviewing a translation, is concerned not so much with its accuracy, but with a literary tradition of engagement with the classics, with a Homer for

---

discussion; Montagu Butler (1913: 27–8) is an early bibliography of such collections.) In the same year, smaller volumes of versions were also published by F. K. Harford, C. H. Bousfield and W. W. Waddell, as well as selections from the *Oxford Magazine*, and poems printed in memoirs such as that of Christopher Wordsworth (my thanks to David Butterfield, who drew my attention to these further volumes). Chris Stray has also reminded me of Frederick Traherne Rickards, who never went to university but did study at school under J. B. Mayor. Rickards worked for the railways in India and produced privately 12 volumes of Greek and Latin prose translations (including of company chairman's speeches). The University of Aberdeen has *90* volumes of translations Rickards collected.

[69]*CR*, 4 (1890: 479).

[70]*CR*, 4 (1890: 263–6, quotations from 266).

the contemporary world, with what a readership for a translation might be. It is a question of the culture of Hellenism in modernity. This single volume of *Classical Review* thus gives a multifaceted picture of the integral role of translation in the broad classical community, from the nitty-gritty of teacher's aids, through the display of civilized skill, to the professional insistence on the precisions of philology, to the construction of privileged cultural genealogy and value. Translation is a fundamental exercise not just of education into classical languages, but of how the classical past can speak to contemporary society.

For this network of scholars and teachers – and it is an interconnected, intergenerational, international elite of educated men, who wrote to and about each other – to write verse translations in Latin and Greek is an exercise in the full sense of *askesis*. It is part of the formation of a cultured self, a means of articulating the bonds that form the network, a mode of public and private expressivity. It is a learned skill, self-consciously privileged, and one that is embodied: Jebb, most famously, like Wordsworth, walked and composed his metrical lines, foot work. It is an act, like praying, playing sport, eating certain foods, that however more sophisticated it becomes over time, always takes the writer back to school days. Montagu Butler – again – recalled visiting Vaughan in Wales just before his former headmaster died. 'During the long hours that followed on that melancholic day, I occupied myself with one more Latin Exercise for the dear and honoured Master to whom I owe so much. I knew that he at least would accept it with indulgence.'[71] The final gift of a translation marks the passing of a Master who became a friend, a final exercise of the skill in which their relationship had been articulated, an emotional transfer to mark the passing of a lifetime of friendship. The reception of the gift, written designedly for one reader's attention, is its very

---

[71]Montagu Butler (1914: ix).

point. We could not be further from the 'invisibility of the translator', the ideal of transparency analysed by Lawrence Venuti as key to the history of translation.[72] Translation is an object as well as a process of exchange.

iii Double vision

Yet, for my purposes in this chapter, the single most important aspect of this pervasive discourse of translation is the *double vision* it requires and expects. For sure, there were many aspirational readers, then as now, who needed translations of Greek and Latin classics to get any access to the otherwise unreadable texts of history, philosophy or poetry of Greece and Rome; there was also a discussion (then as now) about the political virtue of increasing access to the study of classics by bringing classics in translation to classes of men otherwise debarred from the educational system's higher echelons, particularly through teaching for working men's associations. Yet, for the educated readers of *Classical Quarterly*, whether reading English translations of classical literature or reading Greek or Latin translations of English, both languages necessarily and repeatedly echo in and through each other. Walter Headlam, close friend of Virginia Woolf who expressed herself so tellingly on 'not knowing Greek', hints at one understanding of this doubleness. When he turns the prose of the Wisdom of Solomon into Greek verse (as we noted), he points out in an introductory note that the 'only literary value is to point out likenesses of mood and manner in two languages'.[73] For him – and his self-deprecation is certainly disingenuous: he did after all decide to publish this long piece – it is the ability of translation to veil differences in

[72]Venuti (1995).
[73]*CR*, 17 (1903: 367).

similarity that gives translation value. The evident difference of expressivity between ancient languages and modern English becomes a site to demonstrate the process of assimilation. Yet, such performances of translation are not merely the construction of a tradition of classicism, nor only the recognized expertise of elite education. They also allow – require – that both languages are 'put powerfully in motion' by each other (to revert to Benjamin's sense of mobilization). When Montagu Butler republished his *Classical Review* version of 'Crossing the Bar', he started with an extensive essay exploring the grammatical ambiguity of the poem's English and his changing understanding of it.[74] He followed this essay with no fewer than twenty-one versions of Tennyson's poem in Latin and Greek in different metres (and idioms). 'I was constantly haunted,' he writes 'by the conviction that each Metre had, more or less, a personality of its own.'[75] Such translations precisely reveal the inner structures of both languages to each other, and dramatize such recognition of difference: an echoing, reverberating conversation, rather than any greater or purer language. There is no question of 'capturing the original' or veiling difference: here the multiplicity of expressivity and thus comprehension is the very space of cultural performance. It is a performance in *haunted language.*

Victorian Greek and Latin verse translation expect the reader to read *between* Greek or Latin and English, usually with both languages in columns next to each other to aid such double vision. Consider this translation by J. I. Beare, Professor of Greek (previously of Moral Philosophy) at Trinity College, Dublin, published in the *Classical*

---

[74]Montagu Butler (1914: 298–309). Of the English translation of the Bible, he wrote: 'The translation surpasses the original. We not only keep, we also gain' (1913: 17). Wright (1882) consists of 182 translations of Tennyson's epitaph on Sir John Franklin into multiple languages, including Sanskrit and Arabic.
[75]Montagu Butler (1914: vii).

Review for 1906.[76] (Beare also had a couple of poems in *Dublin Greek
and Latin Verses* but his main interest was in philosophy.) Under the
heading 'Version', we are given a scene from Shakespeare's *King John*.
Here are just a few lines of it, with the translation into the expected
Greek iambics:

> *Const.* Yes, that I will; and wherefore will I do it?
> I tore them from their bonds and cried aloud
> 'O that these hands could so redeem my son,
> As they have given these hairs their liberty!'
> But now I envy at their liberty,
> And will again commit them to their bonds,
> Because my poor child is a prisoner.

> καὶ κάρτ' ἔγωγε · πρὸς τί δ'; ἥτις ἄρτι μὲν
> βίᾳ σφε δεσμῶν ἔσπασ', ἔκ τ' ἦυσ' ἅμα
> 'εἴθ' ὥσπερ αἵδε τάσδε λύουσιν τρίχας
> χεῖρες σθένοιεν ὧδε καὶ λύειν τέκνον.'
> νῦν δ' αὖ λυθεισῶν τῶν τριχῶν φθόνος μ' ἔχει
> δεσμοῖσι δέ σφε τοῖς πρὶν ἐνδήσω πάλιν,
> φρονοῦσα παῖδ' ὥς ἐστι δεσμώτης τάλας.

The translation knows that, unlike English which needs its verbs
('I will', 'will I do it?'), Greek will express itself through particles,
pronouns and conjunctions ('καὶ κάρτ' ἔγωγε· πρὸς τί δ';', 'Certainly
I' ... 'Towards what?' Contrast Neoptolemus' stridently emphatic and
consequently tragic ἴτω· ποιήσω, 'Enough! I will take action!' Soph
Phil 120). It also knows that where English is content with an
adversative ('But ...'), Greek will make a contrast (ἄρτι μὲν ... νῦν
δ' αὖ, 'Recently, on the one hand ... But as things now are, on the other

[76]*CR*, 20 (1906: 234).

hand'). Where English uses a subordinate clause ('As ...'), Greek prefers the openness of the genitive absolute participle construction (λυθεισῶν τῶν τριχῶν). In the English, the connection 'because' could be read in various ways: the Greek, by adding the expected participle (φρονοῦσα), makes the connection specific, 'because *I am conscious that* ...'. The English verb of affect 'I envy' becomes an externalized emotion that takes over the subject, φθόνος μ᾽ἔχει, 'Envy possesses me.' Each of these gestures of idiomatic transfer is absolutely familiar, not least from handbooks of Greek composition. As we read *between* the Greek and the English, as the page layout asks, the tensions in the English grammar and the possible solutions in the Greek reveal the inner logic of each language, and, contrary to Benjamin's alienated expectation, dissolve the foreignness of each in mutual interaction and recognizability. Shakespeare, the English bard *par excellence*, the embodiment of the status of the English language as imperial force, is transferred into a version of Greek tragedy, for the admiration of its English-speaking audience. With an echo of Horace's celebrated *bon mot* about victorious Rome's subordination to Greek culture, the original is 'captured' (or not) in translation. But, as with Rome's elite bilingual culture, reading here enacts an exchange between languages that opens both to philological scrutiny and to self-awareness. Reading is conducted with an eye on the other.

Montagu Butler's final 1914 publication of twenty-one Latin and Greek versions of Tennyson's 'Crossing the Bar', an expansion of his single version from 1890, set as it was within his friends' competing translations in Greek and Latin, can be seen therefore not so much as an outstanding display of virtuosity, but rather as a paradigm of this double reading. Each of his versions reveals a new reading of the potential of Tennyson's English; each version set against Tennyson's English reveals a particular 'personality' – a deep structure of philological and cultural expressivity – within the resources of Greek and Latin. The translator and the reader inhabit the in-between of languages, and experience the aesthetic and, above all, epistemological pleasure of shuttling between languages, not seeking, as Benjamin would have it, the 'greater language' or the single, settled voice of the sacred text, but revelling in the multiplicity of voice that the transfers and exchanges of translation afford. Could it be that Henry Montagu Butler, Headmaster of Harrow and Master of Trinity, embraces the ludic openness of language more lovingly than the arch-priest of modernist theory, Walter Benjamin?

The range of texts to be translated – from the greats of Milton, Shakespeare, Browning, Tennyson to the designedly small-beer of 'Black-Eyed Susan' or 'Three Jolly Post Boys', – is thus also not merely to demonstrate the translators' virtuosity. It also states that there is nothing that cannot become part of the classical tradition, whose ideological values underlie the educational system that produces this phenomenon of translation as a privileged cultural achievement. It makes English parallel to Greek and Latin as the authoritative languages of established cultural tradition: a national language. 'We are all (translatable into) Greek . . .,' as Shelley did not quite write. Or, as Shakespeare did write of Bottom in *Midsummer Night's Dream*, 'thou art translated'.

Translation flares into particular significance as a form of cultural expression when cultural tradition and affiliation is under particularly intense stress. For Philo, trying to find the linguistic theory to underpin his desire for cultural hybridity, how Greek-speaking Jews fitted into Alexandria and the tradition of Greek learning was an insistent question. In late antiquity, when, as we mentioned, both Augustine was obsessively reflecting on the language of self-expression against his intellectual anxiety about God's timelessness, and the practice of paraphrase and re-translation of scriptural texts became a

newly important genre in the Roman West and Greek East, such
literary and theological activity must be understood as a response to
how the developing Church should relate to Greek cultural excellence,
now that the Empire was Christian. For the elite, trained in Greek
paideia, the language of the Church needed translating. In the
Reformation, translation was at the heart of the violent conflict over
religion – the very sense of self and the politics of authority within a
nation – that convulsed Europe. How, then, should we understand the
moment that the Victorian practice of Greek verse composition,
typified by Montagu Butler, Jebb, Campbell, Beare and their chums in
the *Classical Review*, represents?

This is not the place for a comprehensive history of the last decades
of the nineteenth century and the opening decades of the twentieth,
but at least some salient vectors can be outlined to help understand
the phenomenon I have been describing. In the most general terms, it
is by now a familiar story that in the nineteenth century, from romantic
Philhellenism through the role of classics in education and classicism
in the arts, to the politics of imperialism, how modern Europe placed
itself in a genealogy with the past of antiquity formed a crucial nexus
of self-definition. Classics – knowing Greek and Latin – was, as the
arch-priest of modernism T. S. Eliot insisted, of paramount concern
for anyone who wished to see a Christian civilization continue.[77]
Translation, as we have seen, played a key role in how the genealogy
that is 'the classical tradition' could be performed by the educated elite
within this politics of self-understanding. We could easily have added
for a contrasting picture the role of, say, Voss's translations of Homer
in how German-speaking classicists explored the connections of the
German national destiny and the deep Greek past. But I would like to
suggest a further more precise connection to the history of education,

---

[77]Martindale (1995).

in which the practice of verse composition of this sort has to be located.

After the 1867 Reform Act, education in Britain was widely expanded, and increasing literacy and compulsory schooling brought to the fore questions of what should be taught in schools and how. Matthew Arnold, whose day job was Schools Inspector, as we have seen, wrote reports both on German Universities and on the place of English rather than classical learning for the widening public for education.[78] Arnold, of course, loved Greek and placed Hellenism at the centre of his value system; but he was clear that for the populace, an education into English first and foremost was required to form an English citizen capable of playing a proper role in the modern nation state. One compelling overarching narrative in the history of the discipline of classics in Britain is its increasing association over the course of the nineteenth century with conservative commitments to tradition and elite schooling. The thrilling opportunity for political revolution that Romantic Philhellenism found in Greek freedom, and the excitement in democracy that the liberal George Grote found in the history of Greece in the mid-century, or the passion for change that Marx saw in the Roman dress of the French Revolution, were transformed into an educational bastion to set against the frightening prospects of violent change that so worried or inspired Europeans, especially after the convulsive and failed revolutionary activity of 1848. (How the potential for revolutionary change through the classical past was displaced into sexual revolution or aesthetics is another narrative, to which we will return.) The separation of classics as an education for the public schools rather than the state schools increasingly worked to make classics a sign of class and status, which the public schools happily promoted. Alongside the professionalization of the discipline of

---

[78]Goldhill (2002: 213–31), Collini (1994) and Connell (1950).

classics, partly in response to the growth and dominance of the German university system, and alongside the increasing status and authority of the public school system in the imagination as well as the educational structure of the nation – the image of Matthew Arnold's father as headmaster of Rugby is iconic here – there grew an increasing fascination with the proper training for the young of the nation. There were more heated and more extensive discussions about education than in any previous period, often focused on the tensions between Classics and science or Classics and theology or Classics and modernity. Classics as a field perceived itself – not for the first or last time – to be under threat. As the position it then held in the curriculum was indeed destined not to be maintained, classics was right to see a challenge to its authority growing.

One response to these vectors that challenged and reasserted the authority of a classical education, was an increasing insistence on *discrimination*. Education at school and university became obsessed with prizes, ranking, scoring – and stories of triumphs in academic competition (or sports or politics or ...) appear and are circulated in biographical narrative after biographical narrative.[79] Verse composition takes on a specific shape within this narrative: within the broad class narrative of an education into classics, composition becomes the distinction of the elite within the elite. Here is how the genial Montagu Butler expresses it:

> There is no greater waste of time than the enforcement of verse-making, whatever the language, where there is no taste for verses to start from. It not only wastes time which might be well employed in many other directions, but it bores, it irritates, it disgusts, it leads to a deep-seated and demoralising scepticism as to the value and

---

[79] I should declare my *parti pris* here: the prize endowed by Montagu Butler for a long hexameter poem in Latin paid for my holiday in Greece in 1977.

the genuineness of all kinds of early mental drill. No, let those of us who contend that for many minds early verse-making, well taught by lively, cultured, sympathising teachers, has a remarkable power to call out intelligence, joyful labour, and ever increasing enthusiasm, let us be the first to admit that we are thinking not of average pupils, nor again by any means of all pupils of distinguished ability, but of what we may call 'chosen vessels', boys and girls who are keenly sensible to the beauties, the graces, the sublimities of literature and specially of Poetry and not only to the value of the thoughts and the truths that it enshrines and explains, but also, in a high degree, to the charms of its expression.[80]

Butler recognizes that not everyone can achieve what verse composition offers (he calls those who cannot learn Greek or Latin properly, 'incurables').[81] But, with the right natural qualities – the inevitable disavowing ground rule of social distinction – and good teachers (a little self-praise), the necessity of 'joyful labour' (a Protestant value if ever there were one) and 'early mental drill', the insistence of Victorian educational theory – then 'chosen vessels' may be selected and achieve the heights of achievement in the 'sublimities of literature'. Butler, it is worth noting, includes girls in this 'joyful labour': in reality, very few girls indeed learned verse or even prose composition, let alone entered the competitions.[82] This was a boys

---

[80]Graham (1920: 367). Gildersleeve (1930: 23), puts this more negatively, of course: 'the fearful waste of time in the classical schools of England, in which the prime of boyhood is spent over the composition of execrable Greek and Latin verses ... In order that one boy may improve a knack in versification, five hundred are sent out without a decent knowledge of Latin prose composition.'
[81]Montagu Butler (1913: 3).
[82]Montagu Butler was married to Agnata Ramsay, who was famous for being the only person to achieve top-class honours in the Cambridge Classics Tripos in 1887: there was a *Punch* cartoon celebrating her achievement. Agnata was surprising also in that, after her marriage, she went on to publish a schools edition of Herodotus 7. When they married, he was 57, she was 21. Apparently, the couple 'read a great deal of Greek together' on their honeymoon (Butler 1925: 32). Prins (2017) is excellent background here.

club. Both the logic and the values of his argument are strikingly expressed. Verse composition is not for all because only some – 'we few, we happy few' – can be chosen.

Here, then, we can vividly see a further cultural politics that underlies the educational practice and subsequent public display of verse composition: an *askesis* to create and display an elite to itself and the public. Such writing is not the literature of 'urgency, assertion and defiance' so often privileged by literary criticism (and embodied in the violent conflict over translation in the early modern era), but a training in mastery, hierarchy, elitism, embedded in the logic of imperialism. It is not by chance that the exams for the imperial Indian Civil Service awarded twice as many marks for knowledge of Greek and Latin than knowledge of native languages, or, indeed, any modern languages.[83] The discrimination of verse composition was a gesture of elite training to set against the surging of class in Britain, always marked by accent and language use, and the multilingual empire.

Where Benjamin saw no place for cultural politics in translation, and declared the insistence on the singularity of meaning in sacred texts to be a transcendent if impossible ideal for translation, the examples I have been discussing show a different route to understanding translation. First, in contrast to the common insistence that the essence of translation is the transfer from ST to TT, source text to translation text, we see from these Victorian practices how the double reading of composition shuttles comprehension between languages, allowing the recognizability of difference, and inhabiting the space of difference – with pleasure in the exploration and negotiation of difference. There are twenty-one ways – and counting – that we can read Tennyson's English through Latin and Greek, and twenty-one ways (and counting)

---

[83]Vasunia (2013).

that Tennyson reveals the personality of Latin and Greek metres as form. Plurality, not singularity, is valued: in contrast to Benjamin's imagined, sacred 'greater language', 'capturing the original' is a constant and enjoyed game of unending chase, not an insistent teleology. The 'ideal receiver', dismissed from the start by Benjamin, is projected as the reader who finds joy in the difference between languages and its negotiation. This ideal reader is paraded – performed – in the reviews of such translations. Second, however, underpinning this openness is a complex politics of tradition – the unending chase of status and authority. Translation matters most when cultural affiliation and value are a source of anxiety and hope – when cultural authority is in translation. To view translation as solely an epistemological or aesthetic issue is to miss this force. If translation is a 'joyful labour', we should not cease to ask *what* it is labouring towards and *for whom* this labour is. It is not enough, with Benjamin, to silence how translation makes a significant intervention in cultural politics, in the construction of cultural capital.

iv How awkward!

I was one of the last students, I suspect, to get what could be called a Victorian education. My school was designedly modern from its establishment. University College School was founded in 1830 to provide students for University College London, the so-called 'Godless institution in Gower Street', one of the first universities in Britain to be set up without an explicitly religious foundation.[84] The school, like the university, had no chapel or religious underpinnings. Consequently, on major Jewish holidays, the school was half-empty – or so I imagined

---

[84]Usher, Black-Hawkins and Carrick (1981).

from the line of boys I joined, all bringing the same note to the headmaster asking to be excused from school on those festival days. (It was much more palatable for Jews to attend a school without a Christian infrastructure.) 'Rosh Hashana?' 'Rosh Hashana?' 'Rosh Hashana?' the headmaster intoned, without opening the envelopes, as boy after boy gave him their parents' letter. In 1903, the school had moved to Hampstead, then as now, a byword in London for artists, musicians, immigrants, though now it is reserved mainly for the wealthiest and most successful bohemians. When I attended it in the 1970s, the school had a flourishing theatre, which staged jazz concerts good enough to get on national radio, and prided itself on its education in the arts, drama and poetry, and used its connections to bring in performers and writers of international stature which the pupils rather took for granted. It was the 1970s, so the boys – it was then all boys – slouched, long-haired, through the streets ostentatiously carrying LP covers that were competitively evaluated as part of social standing. When Alan Ginsberg came and read his poetry to us, we sat and nodded knowingly, knowing very little.

And yet – and it seems hard in retrospect to put this together with the self-consciously trendy atmosphere and sophisticated ideals of the schooling – the curriculum seems now bizarrely – or wonderfully – old-fashioned. The curriculum still privileged not just the humanities but, as with Montagu Butler's nineteenth-century Harrow, classics. The brightest boys were directed towards classics, followed by history or English, with exception made for mathematicians, who were a class apart. Sciences were reserved for the less flamboyantly intellectual. For O levels – now termed GCSEs, the exams that all English students normally take at sixteen – I studied Latin, Greek, English, French, German, Art, Maths – and a single combined science exam that mixed a bit of physics, a bit of chemistry, a bit of biology: science was no more than a required add-on to the serious work. When I finished school, I could not change a plug (and biology was for the imagination). From fifteen onwards, I studied only Greek, Latin and English literature. Not only was classics the 'top set', but it was expected that unlike other subjects which had a two-year curriculum, classicists, and only classicists, would stay on at the school for three years, because this was the only way a true education could be completed, as we were told repeatedly. The aim was not just to obtain a place at Oxford or Cambridge but to win scholarships to the best colleges at those universities, scholarships awarded on academic achievement, judged through special, particularly challenging entrance exams, that the two universities themselves set and marked. These exams were called entrance exams, and, like many entrances, enforced exclusion. The agonistic spirit that Montagu James loved, lived on: those boys who won scholarships had their names and success inscribed on boards by the school hall; and, with a similar sense of public honour, in those days each year Cambridge and Oxford final degree results in classics were still published in the London *Times*.

Integral to this extended curriculum was not just learning Greek and Latin, and reading what would now be regarded as a university-level amount of ancient texts, but also the art of verse composition. It was presented to us as the epitome of school achievement. Prose was, well, prosaic: flair in prose was encouraged, admired, but limited, inevitably. Translating the *Times* leaders into Ciceronian Latin was drilled as an instruction in the flabbiness of English journalism. But verse allowed for real mastery and understanding. The best pieces of student work were collected, as in the nineteenth century, in a volume called *Flosculus*. Inclusion in the leather-bound, folio-sized book was held up as a holy grail, a rare sign of recognized excellence, setting the happy versifier in a line with generations of students who had gone on to great things (as, again, we were regularly told). We composed verse and prose every week in both languages. We were instructed in the technical language of commentaries – *anaphora, anacolouthon, homoioteleuton* – so that we could describe our verses – and Ovid's or Virgil's – properly. What now seems quite remarkable is that as cynical, dismissive, sarcastic adolescents, we bought into this agenda wholeheartedly. Translating Racine from French into Greek iambics seemed to me to be the beating heart of cultured achievement. Ginsberg, schminsberg.

Everyone has embarrassment stored somewhere in the memory of adolescence – an embarrassment formed in the disjunction between what you think you know now and what you thought you knew then (embarrassment is not only an adolescent memory, of course, but a constant companion for us experts in knowing . . .). My embarrassment here is multiply layered, layer after layer of anxious knowingness. I am all too conscious of the remarkable privilege of being offered an education that was available to so few then or now, but that I, like most adolescents, took for granted at the time. These days, I am acutely conscious that any story of privilege is so much less attractive to contemporary expectations than a story of suffering overcome. (You can see why I did not want to talk of privilege in chapter one). Privilege smacks of unappealing smugness or self-satisfaction, especially if it takes the nasty shape of entitlement (which depends on the instrumental misrecognition of systemic privilege). It was not always so, however. In the proliferation of biographies that marks out the history of nineteenth-century literary culture, there are, of course, many wonderful stories of misery or poverty overcome – Dickens made it a staple of his novels. But the dominant form of the genre offers book after book that unembarrassedly tell a boy's own story of success at an elite school followed by triumphs at university and a life in the Empire – narratives where name-dropping ostentatiously announces the Establishment, as it reproduces itself and revels in retrospective self-recognition ('In my class-room/dinner party/drunken brawl were the future prime-minister/poet laureate/governor of India . . .').[85] My

---

[85]Gagnier (1991), Marcus (1994), Broughton (1999) and Saunders (2010).

discussion of Victorian verse composition as a social practice focuses on the men – almost always men – who are the subjects of such narratives. Privilege is rarely chosen as opposed to given, or granted, or inherited; but to understand – to appreciate – what privilege means needs self-awareness over time. Privilege can't be given back, however. And privilege, however fought for or deserved, never exists without a cost to others. To understand how one comes to stand where one stands should be a work in progress.

Yet, it is particularly embarrassing to admit here that I myself had the sort of education in verse composition which I have been critically scrutinizing, and enjoyed it. ('How awkward,' as I was taught to say by an anthropologist, when faced by particularly blatant cultural contradictions . . .) I was very proud indeed when I wrote a composition that was judged worthy of inclusion in *Flosculus*, and doubly proud that I had written it without even a dictionary, while waiting to bat at a cricket match (I knew the clichés of sang-froid and how to admire the appearance of effortlessness). The British Empire was no longer in its Victorian pomp, and my family had no expectation or history of taking up a place within imperial administration; nor had I inherited what would be recognized in Britain as a place in the upper classes (my father was the first member of my family to have gone to university, as a scholarship boy; my mother left school at 16). It is clearer to me now, that in revelling in verse composition as an achievement I was also beguiled by an image of scholarship, the politics of which I could not yet appreciate. Much like the records in their covers that we zealously carried, there was a certain glamour in what seemed counter-cultural. By the 1970s, Latin or Greek verse composition was already a rarity in school curricula, and certainly not part of the normative cultural expectations. Steam-punk education? As my friend and fellow classicist Renaud Gagné proudly reminisced of his own adolescence, 'I was a punk, and doing classics was an extension of that.' By making this *Aufgabe* part of our engagement with literature and our studies, it felt not so much that a conservative, traditional education was being foisted on us or granted to us, but rather that we were constructing for ourselves a world against the dominant bourgeois trivialities (an all too familiar longing of adolescent self-formation). Oddly enough, writing Latin verse – like choosing obscure music, yelling in feverish political debate, going to small theatres, finding books to love, refusing haircuts – was an integral part of what now seems to be the performative search for distinctiveness. As such, it was also absolutely typical of a certain north London privileged middle-class milieu of the 1970s.

Our classics teacher, Dr Usher – unlike other teachers, he was always known with no more of a nickname than 'the doc' – was exceptional; he had a PhD from Cambridge and he knew Greek and Latin very well; he was charismatic; he set remarkably high standards in philology – he brought the latest edition of the *Journal of Hellenic Studies* into class to discuss articles with us. He was also an *arbiter elegantiae*: he was always traditionally well-dressed in suit, waistcoat and watch-chain; he opined that we should start each day with a Haydn symphony; that we should read all of Jane Austen every year; that we should never write on the first page of a notebook. No doubt, he was consciously offering his hairy, messy adolescent pupils a highly constructed sense of tradition. No doubt, his sense of creating a world for himself was integral to his experience growing up as a gay man when it was still illegal to be gay. We also resisted. In my case, it took the form of leaving school for some months after I had been accepted to Cambridge, to take Italian lessons, hang around London theatres, and read on my own. (I have no idea whether such a plan would be possible these days within the regulatory zeal of modern institutions.) I came back only to take my final examinations. I no longer wanted to sit in class.

To escape class … Is that not also part of education, to get away from the bounds of what you are born into? Of course, education reproduces the Establishment, the norms and privileges that keep society's inequalities in place (and some embrace this sense of order wholeheartedly: entitlement starts young). Nor, as Didier Eribon describes so well, is it possible to escape class without deep emotional stressfulness.[86] Individual social mobility, greatly overemphasized in beloved stories of triumphs over adversity, has made little or no change to systematic deprivation.[87] Yet, without education, where would social change come from? Feminism, gay rights, anti-racist movements start from perceived and experienced injustice, but proceed through shared education – education that changes hearts and minds, and eventually expectations, and (finally) laws. Education is central to culture wars because of the tension between these two trajectories – reproducing social norms and changing social understanding. It becomes a bitter, strident battleground because of the vested interests in both vectors, and the stakes are high.

Despite the violent rhetoric that swirls around, there is also, however, a certain fog in these culture wars, an *opacity*. It would, for example, be easy to see studying Greek and Latin verse composition in a privileged school environment as an education into privilege; since it was part of a process that led in my case to an elite university education and a career in the system, it would indeed be fair to describe it in such a way. But this description would not represent the experience adequately. Rather – or also – to choose such study was part of an attempt to stand aside from dominant cultural expectations, to resist what was seen as conformity – that is, the assumption that education was a route towards financial success, a profession, a job. Doing classics, doing classics *like this*, was willingly to face the question that no lawyer, banker, civil servant was destined to face: why are you doing *that*? As

---

[86]Eribon (2013).
[87]Mandler (2016).

my mother, many years after I had left school and cut my hair, asked her best friend, 'Professor of Greek? What's the good of that?' To choose to devote your life to studying antiquity is to be doubly exiled: you can never live in the place you study, and you can never quite fit into modernity's self-serving demands. Untimeliness is endemic to classics: hence Victorian practices of teaching verse composition in the 1970s. But, also, hence the desire to resist the times. To change the times. Loving classics, however traditional a subject it might seem, can also be a way of stepping off the path, looking elsewhere and otherwise. As Saidiya Hartman knows, it can be essential to find 'fugitive spaces of waywardness'.[88]

v Tradition's claim

The classical tradition – the history of the discipline and its reach – has become a battleground again, as I am writing this. The case of classics is a good example of how the rhetoric over education – over culture as an alibi for inequality – can quickly become very shrill, and forgetful. When Dan-el Padilla Peralta, a professor of Roman history at Princeton, who is Black, was reported to say that if classics as a discipline could not change its relation to exclusionary privilege, it would be better to burn it down, he was both lionized and excoriated, as if there had been no conditional clause in his statement of principle. Many people had been campaigning to promote this agenda over many years. There is a long tradition of classicists committed to political activism, epitomized by Gilbert Murray's contribution to the League of Nations and the international peace movement (he also voted as a professor of Greek for the abolition of compulsory Greek);[89] but, in recent decades, critical

---

[88]Hartman (2019); the phrase itself is from Honig (2021: 71).
[89]Stray, ed. (2007).

race theory at one level, and local activism at another has motivated a roster of classical academics and students.[90] But, helped by a very high-profile profile in the *New York Times Magazine* – and, inevitably, the newspaper's canny manipulation of the Black Lives Matter moment – Dan-el Padilla Peralta became the very visible figurehead for the case for changing the dynamics of inclusivity in Classics. It would be satisfying not to have to pay attention to those few loud and aggressive voices that have tried for their own purposes to ignore the conditional clause that grounds Padilla Peralta's fiery rhetoric. No one should want a crowd, especially a crowd of classicists, to chant, 'Burn it down,' nor are the barbarians at the gate, needing self-righteous heroes to fight them off – or at least the barbarians are not embodied by Dan-el. Padilla Peralta has told his own moving and inspirational story, how he ended up as an undocumented immigrant from the Dominican Republic living on the street in New York, and how studying classics led him to a new life, supported by a fine education thanks to scholarships at excellent private schools.[91] He teaches now at the archetype of American privilege, Princeton. If anyone embodies the tension between education as a preparation to join the elite, and education as a possibility of changing the times, it is Dan-el Padilla Peralta. What Padilla Peralta asks for – and it seems completely reasonable to me – is that the discipline of classics should pay attention to the role it has long played in the construction of privilege and, most importantly, *do* something about it, now.

The urgency of his appeal has deep roots. Martin Luther King Jr. knew that the advice to wait for a change to come was a poisonous encouragement of complicit delay: 'time itself becomes an ally of the forces of social stagnation', he declared in his remarkable testimony,

---

[90]See, e.g. Rankine (2006, 2013), Allen (2004, 2016), McCoskey (2012), Capettini and Rabinowitz, eds (2021) and the many authors who contributed to *Eidolon*'s seven-year life.
[91]Padilla Peralta (2015).

'Letter from a Birmingham Jail' (which would be on my list of compulsory reading for school kids). 'For years now,' Dr King states, 'I have heard the word "Wait!" It rings in the ear of every Negro with piercing familiarity. This "Wait" has almost always meant "Never." We must come to see, with one of our distinguished jurists, that "justice too long delayed is justice denied". These powerful, stirring words were written in 1963, and it is a lasting shame that they are still so pertinent. One of the shocking recognitions of reading the incisively moral words of James Baldwin now – or hearing him in the remarkably moving film, *I Am Not Your Negro* – is how precisely relevant his analysis remains – and thus how little has productively changed.[92] I know from my own work both in the university and on national and international funding and policy committees how unjustifiably slow it has been to move from awkward recognition to significant and instrumental action on shifting the dynamics of exclusion and belonging. Space, the space of privilege, is not ceded easily. Thoughtlessness or lack of awareness can have the same result as purposive action to maintain the status quo – and, as Sara Ahmed has incisively shown, the bland comfort of 'policy statements' is positively ineffective for real change, the surest way, indeed, to keep inequality in place.[93] A discipline that cannot face up to its own history, that cannot act with social responsibility, that cannot recognize a need not just to change with the times, but to change the times, is, indeed, a discipline without a decent future.

Classics, of all disciplines, has a particular investment in its own tradition. Just now, I wrote that the classical tradition 'has become a battleground *again*' because the history of the field is a long narrative

---

[92] *I Am Not Your Negro*, directed by Raoul Peck, is easily available on Netflix; on the relevance of Baldwin, see Glaude (2021).

[93] Ahmed (2021). Fanon ([1952] 2008: 89–119) is extraordinarily complex and moving on 'waiting', as part of the psychological trauma of racism, ending with (119), 'I wait for myself. Just before the film starts, I wait for myself. Those in front of me, spy on me, wait for me.'

of battles over what past is to count and how (a history that has been inadequately acknowledged in much of the current debate). The high points should be familiar. The Renaissance was the rediscovery of the classical, and especially the Greek past, but it was a discovery that was instrumental in the religious and political polemics of the Reformation. Erasmus' iconic admonition for scholars to return *ad fontes*, to the sources of Christianity written in Greek (and Hebrew), led to the recognition not just that Jerome's Latin translation, long authorized by liturgical use and everyday reading, was open to serious question, but also that the very texts themselves were precariously established, with interpolations and mis-readings uncontested.[94] The intellectual and physical violence of the subsequent religious polemics led to the foundation of the Protestant churches, and the Counter-Reformation's restatement of principle at the Council of Trent, where Jerome's Vulgate was declared 'authentic', a translation that was the true word of God. It was possible for a cleric in the midst of this turmoil to write – a burn-it-down moment – that learning Greek was *heresy*. For him you would, indeed, *burn in hell* if you encouraged Greek verse composition. How could learning the language in which the Gospels were written put your mortal soul at risk?

In the later cultural strife of the Enlightenment, the so-called *querelle* of ancients and moderns, dominated European-wide arguments over value – over what lasts or must change in the Church and in culture, especially.[95] For the *modernes*, to write classicizing verse, as Racine did, was an aesthetic and political misprision of the demands of modernity (and to translate it into Greek would only be to double the error). What was at stake in the *querelle* was authority in and of the past, and the possibility of changing the times. Was

---

[94]Goldhill (2002: 14–60, with bibliography).
[95]Bullard and Tadié, eds (2016).

knowledge an incremental process, 'standing on the shoulders of giants', as the revolutionary Newton insisted? Or was the here and now an era of transformative disruption? As Swift's 'Battle of the Books' satirically dramatizes, these questions turned to violent disagreement ('Pindar … with a mighty stroke, cleft the wretched Modern in twain'). To determine a place in history was also to contest the potential of making a break with the past: to argue about tradition was to fight about the very direction of society.

In the following centuries, as classics grew to become the dominant discipline of nineteenth-century educational institutions, and philology 'the queen of the sciences',[96] there was also a bitter challenge to the place of classics, a challenge in the name of 'useful knowledge' and the material understanding of the world. Throughout the century in which classics was central to the curriculum, 'Who needs Greek?' became a question explicitly debated as Greek and then Latin were finally declared no longer to be compulsory training for an elite university education.[97] Knowing how to write Greek was attacked as the epitome of useless knowledge. The place of classics in the curriculum could be expunged. 'Exclude Greek' from the curriculum, concluded Henry Sidgwick, guru of reform at Cambridge.[98] 'No liberal mind will regret [its] abolition,' wrote another liberal nineteenth-century professor of Greek:[99] burn it down …

This whistle-stop tour of what could obviously be a more complex and more extended narrative is to emphasize one simple point: although tradition often represents itself – masquerades – as stable, immutable, uncontroversial, there has in fact been a long history of

---

[96]Kurtz (2021).
[97]Goldhill (2002: 178–245).
[98]Sidgwick (1867: 141).
[99]Sellar (1867: 7).

often bitter, violent and society-changing argument about what the classical tradition means and what its status is, in education, culture, self-understanding. And so, for us now, too – rightly.

Tradition, to paraphrase Heidegger, is a rhetoric designed to present the past as self-evident – an ideological projection that determines not only which past is to be authorized, but also how the present finds its own genealogy in the past. The claim of tradition – a commonplace in education as in religion – acts upon society to keep things as they are. Tradition is not a given, but always needs to be constructed, asserted, maintained – performed. It is a way of authoritatively locating oneself in the present by determining that such an authority, such a sense of placement, comes from a historically privileged continuity: a line, an ancestry, a promise. Tradition not only presents the past as self-evident but brings with it a set of normative claims about value, status and belonging. Tradition is how cultural ideology writes its history.

Tradition becomes a matter of debate when *fitting in* has become a pressing issue; when rupture from the past demands attention and produces dissent; when cultural ideology begins to fracture. Then tradition becomes turbulent. A stimulus to and place for conflict, rather than a strut and stay of belonging. Dan-el Padilla Peralta's insistence on the need for change (he is far from alone in this) is because simply to continue in the same way as in the past has become intolerable, because the established – traditional – privilege of education comes at too great, too *damaging* a cost to too many underprivileged members of society, to society as a whole. The professional discipline of classics can and should take a lead in this project of needed transformation.

The demand to 'decolonize the classics' – the current banner – insists that the tradition that enshrines the texts of the classical canon must be overturned, in the belief that curriculum reform would be the first step in this project of transformation. (The call for curriculum change in classics departments would be a very small, even parochial step if it did not raise further more stressful questions.) One argument is that these ancient texts are complicit with the masters of imperialism, colonialization, sexism, racism, especially in the nineteenth century when classics took shape as a discipline and dominated the curriculum of elite education. The powers of Empire found or adopted ancestors; the texts of this privileged past authorized present mastery: the canon is the rule of rulers. 'Historicism,' for which classics provided a privileged paradigm, 'enabled European domination of the world in the nineteenth century,' wrote Dipesh Chakrabarty, already twenty years ago.[100] Thomas Babington Macaulay can stand as an icon of this case: he travelled out to rule India as part of the British Empire, where he would write his now infamous *Minute on Indian Education*, condemning the literary culture of the subcontinent: on the ship out, he read Virgil and Livy to prepare himself for the task ahead.[101] Back in Oxford, Benjamin Jowett tutored the future rulers of empire through his classes in classics.[102] There can be no doubt that the institutionalization of classics runs hand in hand with a European imperial project, and, for the British, paradigmatically, the classical antiquity of Greece and Rome was used to bolster the privilege of white, Anglo-Saxon dominance. 'The world is a world for the Saxon race,' as Martin Farquhar Tupper, Queen Victoria's favourite poet, wrote, in ringing celebration of the naturalness of Empire. How the world *just is* . . .

But this is only part of the story. There are also familiar counter-cases who discovered in classics a revolutionary, liberational force – and who changed society. A decent intellectual history of our own

---

[100]Chakrabarty (2000: 7), a case extended now by Satia (2020).
[101]Hall (2012) and Vasunia (2013).
[102]Dowling (1994).

tradition also demands acknowledgement of these figures, not to rest comfortably on historical laurels of past significance – another ruse to avoid looking at the here and now – but to recognize the full potential of the classical past for contemporary engagement. Karl Marx, who completed his PhD in classics, insisted that the French Revolution, with its principles of liberty, equality, and fraternity, was 'enacted in Roman dress'. (It may be fashionable in some quarters to be blasé or sniffy about Marx and Marx's classical interests, or Freud, for that matter, but such a dismissive attitude is trivial and, in truth, silly. The making of modernity is unnarratable without these scholars, inspired by antiquity as they were.) The American revolutionaries, too, saw themselves as following principles they had learnt from the classics. It was, insisted conservative critics, too dangerous to allow the young to read Thucydides, lest democratic revolt take hold. Plutarch, Bernard Shaw summed up happily from his left-wing perspective, was a 'revolutionists' handbook',[103] (a promise perhaps not totally fulfilled by today's International Plutarch Society).When Shelley claimed, 'We are all Greeks,' it was a clarion call to political revolution, which many took up (or wished to from their armchairs).[104] Classical antiquity provided an idealized view of the past that grounded, justified, inspired hopes for change to a better world. Consequently, how Greek history itself should be understood – whether through the liberal George Grote's celebration of democracy or through Mitford's hatred of it – became a major political as much as an educational issue of the nineteenth century. Classics inspired political revolution: the will to move from how the world *just is* towards *justice* (as Amanda Gorman would say).

Such contentiousness brought classics into conflict with Christianity and its institutions, too (as with the Reformation and the

---

[103]Cited Jones (1974: 136).
[104]Wallace (1997).

Enlightenment) – to the extent that philology, 'the queen of sciences', could be lambasted as 'the Antichristian conspiracy'.[105] Gibbon's, *History of the Decline and Fall of the Roman Empire*, was bowdlerized (literally, by Thomas Bowdler) because chapters 15 and 16 offered such a cynical and damaging view of the evidence for miracles in the Gospels that his history was seen as a scoffing attack on Christianity.[106] Classical scholarship – reading Homer in a modern, that is, nineteenth-century theoretically-informed way – 'ushered in scepticism in the Old Testament', or so the great churchman, Edward Pusey, declared with deep anxiety.[107] When William Gladstone, the prime minister of Britain, wrote a long pamphlet trying to show rather that the Hebrew Bible and Homer could be reconciled as evidences of God's providence in the world, it sold over 120,000 copies.[108] Many shared Pusey's anxiety, it would seem, and wanted the counter-case, and from an authority such as the prime minister. At this level of intellectual activity, classics and theology had its dances, disruptive or cheek to cheek;[109] at quite another level, the promise of antiquity also fuelled the hopeful renegades of 'new paganism', 'the myth of the goddess' – other routes towards the divine, a different story of the self.[110]

Classics was the inspiration for aesthetic revolution also, and not just with the philhellenic poets such as Shelley. Richard Wagner, the most contentious and influential of nineteenth-century grandees of spectacular performance, when he wrote his programmatic treatise *Art and Revolution*, took his grounding and idealistic hope from ancient Greece. Wagner pronounced he would rather be a Greek in the theatre

---

[105]Lockhart (1850: 437). 'Queen of sciences' is from Kurtz (2021: 752), which is excellent on the history of philology; see also Daston and Most (2015) and Turner (2014).
[106]Turner (1981) remains the best discussion of this.
[107]Pusey (1854: 62).
[108]Gange (2009).
[109]Conybeare and Goldhill, eds (2020).
[110]Louis (2005).

of Dionysus for a single day than live for ever. His 'music of the future' was a revolution based on an ideal vision of an ancient Greek past, which Nietzsche shared: a memory of a place not yet found.[111] For many others, Greece offered a hope of sexual revolution – whether through Freud's Oedipus or Wilde's 'philosophizing'. Sexology's casebook starts in antiquity. When the American Senate debated the commissioning of Vinnie Ream, a young woman, to make a statue of Lincoln, it was Sappho the senators reached for to argue the case (Ream went on to make a sculpture of Sappho ...).[112] The image of a city where males could desire males without moral opprobrium, or where Sappho was an honoured artist, was a dream (in all senses) that has continued to fire the ongoing fight for gay and feminist rights into the twenty-first century. It is not by chance that both Judith Butler and Bonnie Honig have turned back to Greek tragedy to rewrite an idea of kinship and of feminist refusal.[113] Intellectual genealogy matters and enables. For Butler, Hegel is precisely the starting point that leads her to *Antigone*. For feminist thinkers, the history of the Western family finds foundational studies in Bachofen's *Mutterrecht* and, after Bachofen, in Engels and other Marxist writing on property and inheritance, which lead in turn to Simone de Beauvoir's and Luce Irigaray's readings of Aeschylus' *Oresteia* in particular and Greek myth in general as the struts of patriarchy, which need to be pulled down. 'Heterotopias' are how we can explore our desires, 'practice how to be otherwise, and reimagine what the world might be': that's Bonnie Honig, riffing on the work of Bernice Johnson Reagon, searching for a 'conceptual life of promising spaces'.[114] Is not the classical antiquity of Greece or Rome such a heterotopia? A space of

[111]Goldhill (2011: 125–52).
[112]Cooper (2009).
[113]Butler (2002) and Honig (2021).
[114]Honig (2021: 70); 'The Conceptual Life of Promising Spaces' is the subtitle of Cooper (2013).

imagining the world otherwise? A resource or potential for recognizing otherness in the world and in yourself?

Yet, this, too, is only part of the story. As Sophocles knew long ago, fierce commitment brings its own blindness. And revolution comes hand in hand with disappointment. The musical and political revolutionary Wagner was also a foul and aggressively active anti-Semite, who wrote that the only way for Jews to enter humanity was by their willed destruction as Jews. Bernard Shaw, notwithstanding his very public socialist values, supported the racist theories of Houston Stuart Chamberlain – a hugely influential theorist, whose dying hands Hitler travelled to kiss: it was Chamberlain who determined that world history was explained by the clash of the pure races of Teutons and Jews, and that the mixed races, above all, were a desecration of society's mission, a disgusting idea that still grounds the more extreme forms of racism.[115] Byron's revolutionary philhellenism came with rapacious sexual compulsions enacted with the unpleasant entitlement of his class. It should produce a salutary caution to see how the heroic class-warrior (say) may be also sexist, the feminist inadequately aware of race. (In the face of such history, you would have to be very self-righteous, and, frankly, pretty un-self-aware, to think your own political commitments are so transparently and comprehensively beyond reproach that no future will find you lacking in some significant respect: however radical, you are still of your time.) It is telling, however, that although racism in its modern form was being actively formulated and contested in the nineteenth century, its engagement by classicists, however revolutionary they might be in other respects, was almost entirely from a perspective that supported a genealogy that justified the supremacy of the culture, authority, and power of the dominant white, Christian, European, male elite.

---

[115]Field (1981).

So, while it is demonstrably false that the study of classical literature and culture has been or is *inherently* or *necessarily* associated solely with political, social or cultural conservatism, the institutions and practices of the discipline, as with society as a whole, must do a lot more work to change if they are not now to be open to such accusations. Classics opens the door to another place, a place often idealized, which creates a space for the imagination of a better world: this can be a conservative rejection of the modern world, it can be a revolutionary charge to change the modern world. The tension between the two trajectories *together* drives the rich history of the discipline. And for many classicists, that tension is an integral part of our lived experience: the classicists who want the field to change also chose to be classicists. And unlike my choice, overdetermined by my schooling, those who choose classics at university do so decisively. ('We will choose Sophocles,' writes Mahmoud Darwish, arrestingly, lining Palestinian cultural aspirations with Matthew Arnold.)[116] This internalized conflict is not a paradox or something to sneer at, but an essential recognition of the complexity of asking of *how* we fit into tradition, now.

Recognizing this long and continuing politics is a necessary part of the responsibility of academia – to the past, the present and the future. It is because the tradition of our discipline is so conflicted and complex that it can be made to tell many partial stories: that is how cultural ideology tells history. The responsibility to narrate this history – and to narrate it as well as possible – remains pressing, as a necessary agenda of self-understanding, as part of the necessary development of the discipline. Recognizing the continuity of the blindness of the past into the present also requires responsible action in response.

Like Christianity – less often discussed as such by classicists, who do not seem to have read Baldwin's *The Fire Next Time*, but more often than

---

[116]Darwish (2011: 83–7).

classics the driving force of invading and colonizing the territory of
others, as well as more internal disavowals of oppression – like
Christianity the discipline of classics certainly was intertwined with
imperialism and racism and sexism especially in the nineteenth century.
Like the Church (Catholic or Protestant) and all branches of academic
study, for so long institutionally integrated with the Churches, classics
has a long history of claims of universalism, which are undermined by
institutional and systematic exclusion of women, people of colour,
non-European communities. For every story of a life transformed
through education and aspiration, there is a story of complicity,
marginalization and the sociopolitical consequences of such exclusion.
While Catholics, Jews and women – in that order – have gradually been
allowed into what remain dominantly Protestant universities, the actual
process of moving from 'toleration' – the legal ban on exclusion – to lack
of discrimination is an even slower movement, full of disavowals and
disappointments and denigrations. For other historically disadvantaged
communities, it is even slower still, shamefully so. The institutions of
classics have not transcended nor even militated successfully against the
unacceptable expectations of what remains a racist society. Like Dan-el
Padilla Peralta, I would like to think they – we – can.

A properly nuanced history of classics as a discipline, therefore,
should make tradition anything but self-evident. Indeed, Hugh Lloyd-
Jones, Christopher Stray, or Phiroze Vasunia tell the history of our
discipline quite differently . . . For Lloyd-Jones, the discipline of classics
is a roll call of Great Men, facing the same problems of philology over
time, in a sort of ahistorical conversation of scholar to scholar to . . .
Lloyd-Jones: insider dealing, no guests invited.[117] For Christopher
Stray, who loves the prosopography of the discipline in another way,

---

[117]Lloyd-Jones' introduction to Wilamowitz-Moellendorf (1982), following the example of
Pfeiffer (1968, 1976).

institutional history with its connection to government policy, and the enactment of policy from school to university, and its embedding in publishing and scholarly practices, reveals the shape of the discipline through its sociological formation – though Stray's sociology is for my taste too calmly divorced from the sweep of war, cultural clash and economic disaster (and would look different outside Britain, too, of course).[118] For Phiroze Vasunia, who also carefully records the formation and deformation of the scholars he includes in his account, the discipline's story involves a narrative of race and empire, strategies of epistemological and political imposition.[119] Constanze Güthenke, mind you, to break the roll call of men on men, adds the collaboration of *symphilology* to the picture of our disciplinary practices – as a critique of the scholarly tradition about scholarly tradition.[120] We could and should include the intimate connection and dislocation of classics and theology, where 'tradition' becomes fully charged with the assertion of the Catholic Church to 'the apostolic succession' and the Protestant resistance to such assertiveness.[121] This, even before we blend in the distorting frames of class and gender that classics shares with other subjects of study.

Tradition is a constant story of fighting over what past is to count and how, what narrative to tell (though all such narratives are about self-placement, self-justification). What you read matters to who you are or want to become – we are all heirs of the Humboldtian ideal, which made the *Bildung* of its students a rationale of the university – their formation as civilized, cultured subjects. Yet *how* one reads also makes all the difference – as every feminist, faced by the texts of patriarchy, knows. We read *between* identification and resistance,

---

[118]See especially the seminal Stray (1998), also Stray, ed. (1999).
[119]Vasunia (2013).
[120]Güthenke (2020).
[121]Conybeare and Goldhill, eds (2020).

between attachment and distance, *between* criticism and affirmation, recognitions of difference and recognitions of sameness. And nowhere more so than when we read texts of Greek and Latin antiquity which, by definition, are another world to all of us. The question is how to negotiate this otherness of the past, what it is to mean to us.

When Nietzsche declares he is becoming more Greek day by day in his body – as if! – it is easy to see how fantasy drives the desire for the classical – to belong, to see oneself in the other world of antiquity or as its heir. Yet, how can we not recognize that modern philosophy remains integrally and fundamentally in debt to its Platonic foundations? To do philosophy is to speak Greek (as Derrida put it). On the one hand, then, we can see the continuing power of the past over contemporary intellectual formation: the past matters to who we are, who we have become; on the other hand, we have to interrogate how an imaginary of the past – to see oneself in it and find a genealogy for oneself – is filled with projection and fantasy. A statue of George Washington in a toga embodies that projected, fantasized desire. The complexities of the dynamic between these two recognitions are all too often forgotten in the passions of contemporary politics and the undoubted need for change.

Franz Fanon, whose work has grounded so much revolutionary writing in recent decades, famously wrote: 'Each generation must discover its mission, fulfil it or betray it, in relative opacity' – a powerful sentence which led me to choose the word 'opacity' earlier to describe the fog of culture wars.[122] The call to 'mission' with the emotional anticipation of fulfilment or betrayal (a mixture of Christian evangelicalism and the heroic militarism of *Mission Impossible*?) is stirring, but the added recognition of 'in relative opacity' is a really

---

[122]Fanon ([1961] 2004: 145).

striking and challenging endnote. This opacity is relative in at least two ways, I think, more specific than the unintended consequences that always threaten political choices. Fanon asks us first to think about the earlier generations and their fights, to see one's own struggles relative to those earlier generations, and to recognize how hard it is to maintain a simple, unidirectional teleology of transformation. Fanon recognizes that knowing one's place in history is always marked by a certain opacity. Second, Fanon asks us to recognize the opacity that marks our self-understanding. The consciousness that leads to political commitment should not be mistaken for transparency to oneself, however painful lived experience may be. Fanon's impact – his agency – was opaque even to himself, he knew. What is still so surprising about Fanon's sentence is how his clarion call to 'mission' ends in such 'sober' self-evaluation (Homi Bhabha's adjective).[123] Like Dan-el Padilla Peralta's conditional clause, Fanon's hesitancy grounds his nonetheless stirring and incisive analysis. The maturity of judgement that Fanon allows does not negate his fervour or his critical force. To me, it makes Fanon all the more attractive a thinker.

Disorientation – in the sense that Sara Ahmed mobilizes the concept – should characterize how we respond to (fitting into) the classical tradition.[124] Telling one's own story of becoming a classicist can and should be part of this disorientation, part of the process of turning away towards another perspective, another language, a perspective on alterity. I would hope that any such a narration is not just the assertion of an identity, a claim of rights or privilege, a performance of assuredness, but a mix of anecdotes, self-reflections, jokes – and a refusal of the *just is*. The opacity that Fanon recognizes, along with the history of the classical tradition that I have outlined, reminds us that

---

[123]Bhabha (2021): 'post-colonial political sobriety'.
[124]Ahmed (2006).

the tension between education as an induction to privilege and education as a drive towards change is not just long-lived but also *unending*. This tension can and should be recalibrated, but it cannot be removed. Becoming a classicist is a privilege, for anyone, but it should be obvious that this process of becoming is far from a level playing field, but matches society's inequalities, contingencies and barriers. Learning to write Latin and Greek verse was a privilege, a considerable privilege, given to me, and it has helped me into the privileged position I inhabit. The teaching is in me, in my body in how I react to the rhythm of ancient poetry, its inner structure. But I understand this education differently now from when it was part of my own incipient desire to become a scholar, to live life as a scholar. My still changing comprehension both of the classical tradition's conflicting vectors and of the conflicting vectors of my own experience is part of my repeated (dis)orientation towards a scholar's life. Instrumentality within an academic environment is frequently difficult to parse, ineffectively translated, and driven by complicated self-interests. But such opacity does not excuse anyone from the responsibility of action, nor from self-reflection about their place within the continuing and endemic tension between privilege and change in the discipline of classics. Making a difference should always be a motivation and an aim – to transform the shape of the discipline as well as its habits and achievements.

My life is lived in translation. When authoritarian governments, aggressive technocrats, and blinkered administrators insist that material advancement, with its systemic inequalities and destructiveness, is the necessary and sole route to social progress, the waywardness of choosing classics has never felt more compelling to me. We need its heterotopic potential more than ever. But this waywardness comes for me with a commitment to curating the discipline of classics – passing on the skills and knowledge that the study of antiquity requires; testing, refining, adding. I get upset if my students do not learn enough about metre to understand the internal structuring of the language and form of ancient poetry, even if they do not spend time translating Tennyson into Sapphics. It is *between* waywardness and curation that the awkward life in translation is lived.

Nor does privilege necessarily translate into belonging. Of course, my education comes from and enacts a certain privilege – how could it not? – but education and fitting in do not always go hand in hand. Walter Benjamin, whatever his education and self-awareness, was forced into exile as a consequence of his society's aggression towards Jews, a journey which culminated in his suicide. I am always rather chary of colleagues who profess themselves totally at home in the institutions of classics: they are often the same people who use the word 'tradition' as if it were an uncontested monument (and themselves as its gatekeepers). Not quite fitting in is a form of *recognition* – of self and others – that motivates a commitment to transforming the discipline and oneself in it.[125] For me, this has been a constant process, even as I have become increasingly embedded in the institutions of power – funding agencies, boards, policy units. The danger of institutionalization – its duration as well as its rewards – is to forget the creative thrill of waywardness and turn away from the awkward. A life in translation is also lived *between* belonging and not fitting in, *between* institutional participation, with all its complicities, and a desire for change.

Emma Goldman, quoted fondly by Saidiya Hartman, described her America as plagued by 'an epidemic of virtue', and, as Hartman tells it, so much of the brutal mistreatment of young Black men and women was expressly motivated – agitated – by such proclaimed and enacted virtue, a mask not only of cruelty but also of fearful defence of social

---

[125]See Felski (2021) for the politics of this sense of recognition.

position.[126] It is dismaying to see how often the necessary current debates about the discipline of classics and of the politics of education more generally are distorted by a paraded self-righteousness – an authoritarian proclamation of identity, uprightness, morality. The contingencies and transformations of living in-between tend to get lost in such polarized disputes. Perhaps – and I know this will be open to misunderstanding – we need a little less virtue, and a little more recognition of our wayward, awkward lives in classical translation.

We do a lot of translating in classics. *Translatio linguarum, translatio scientiae, translatio imperii* ... Walter Benjamin knew the potential that the translatability of languages could release, but he also projected an ideal of a purer, transcendent language. It is hard not to be moved by the poignancy of such an imagination when we also recall the violent politics of racial and moral purity that eventually uprooted and overwhelmed his life. But classicists know all too well that there is always another translation possible, and each generation needs its own translations. Translation is always transformational, and the untimely, heterotopic dynamic of classics requires us to keep seeing ourselves and the past otherwise. Translating and transformation go together, and should be embraced at the heart of our work. Classics as a discipline needs its translation.

---

[126]Goldman (1917: 198) and Hartman (2019: 308).

Bibliography

Aciman, A. (2016), 'W.G. Sebald and the Emigrants', *New Yorker*, August 25. Available at: https://www.newyorker.com/books/page-turner/w-g-sebald-and-the-emigrants (accessed 19 July 2021).

Adams, J. (2003), *Bilingualism and the Latin Language*, Cambridge: Cambridge University Press.

Adorno, T. (1993), *Hegel: Three Studies*, trans. S. Nicholsen, Cambridge, MA: MIT Press.

Ahmed, S. (2004), *The Cultural Politics of Emotion*, Edinburgh: Edinburgh University Press.

Ahmed, S. (2006), *Queer Phenomenology: Orientation, Objects, Others*, Durham, NC: Duke University Press.

Ahmed, S. (2012), *On Being Included: Racism and Diversity in Institutional Life*, Durham, NC: Duke University Press.

Ahmed, S. (2017), *Living a Feminist Life*, Durham, NC: Duke University Press.

Ahmed, S. (2021), *Complaint!*, Durham, NC: Duke University Press.

Alexander, M. (2010), *The New Jim Crow: Mass Incarceration in the Age of Color Blindness*, New York: New Press.

Allen, D. (2004), *Talking to Strangers: Anxieties of Citizenship since Brown v. Board of Education*, Chicago, IL: University of Chicago Press.

Allen, D. (2016), *Education and Equality*, Chicago, IL: University of Chicago Press.

Allen, D. (2017), *Cuz: The Life and Times of Michael A.*, New York: Liveright.

Althusser, L. (1971), 'Ideology and Ideological State Apparatuses (Notes Towards an Investigation)', in *Lenin and Philosophy and Other Essays*, trans. B. Brewster, New York: Monthly Review Press.

Ando, C. (1990), 'Augustine on Language', *Révue des études Augustiniennes*, 40: 45–78.

Appiah, K. A. (2005), *The Ethics of Identity*, Princeton, NJ: Princeton University Press.

Appiah, K. A. (2006), *Cosmopolitanism: Ethics in a World of Strangers*, New York: W. W. Norton.

Appiah, K. A. (2014), *Lines of Descent: W.E.B. Du Bois and the Emergence of Identity*, Cambridge, MA: Harvard University Press.

Arendt, H. (1951), *The Origins of Totalitarianism*, New York: Schocken Books.

Arendt, H. (1958), *The Human Condition*, Chicago, IL: University of Chicago Press.

Arendt, H. (1963), *Eichmann in Jersualem: A Report on the Banality of Evil*, New York: Viking.

Arnold, M. (1861), *On Translating Homer: Three Lectures Given at Oxford*, London: Longmans, Green, Longman, and Roberts.

Arnold, M. (1908), *Reports on Elementary Schools, 1832–1882*, London: Macmillan.

Arnold, M. (1960–77), *Complete Prose Works*, 12 vols, R. Super (ed.), Ann Arbor, MI: Michigan University Press.

Asad, T. (2003), *Formations of the Secular: Christianity, Islam, Modernity*, Stanford, CA: Stanford University Press.

Atwood, M. (2005), *The Penelopiad*, London: Canongate.

Auerbach, E. ([1946] 1953), *Mimesis: The Representation of Reality in Western Literature*, trans. W. Trask, Princeton, NJ: Princeton University Press.

Azar, M. G. (2016), *Exegeting the Jews: The Early Reception of the Johannine 'Jews'*, Leiden: E.J. Brill.

Baddiel, D. (2021), *Jews Don't Count*, London: HarperCollins.

Baldwin, J. ([1967] 1969), 'Negroes are Anti-Semitic because They are Anti-White', in *Black Anti-Semitism and Jewish Racism*, J. Baldwin, E. Raab, J. Kaufman, A. W. Miller, W. H. Booth, W. Karp, H. R. Shapiro, H. Cruse, A. Vorspan and J. Lester, with an introduction by N. Hentoff, 3–12, New York: E. P. Dutton. Baldwin's article was originally published in the *New York Times*, 19 April 1967.

Ball, R. (2021), *The Classical Legacy of Gilbert Highet: An In-Depth Retrospect*, Columbus, GA: Lockwood Press.

Bar-On, D. (1989), *Legacies of Silence: Interviews with Children of the Third Reich*, Cambridge, MA: Harvard University Press.

Barker, P. (2018), *The Silence of the Girls*, London: Penguin Books.

Barner, W., and C. König, eds (2001), *Jüdische Intellektuelle und die Philologien in Deutschland, 1871–1933*, Göttingen: Wallstein Verlag.

Barton, C. and D. Boyarin (2016), *Imagine No Religion: How Modern Abstractions Hide Ancient Realities*, New York: Fordham University Press.

Bassnett, S. (2002), *Translation Studies*, New York and London: Psychology Press.

Baumgarten, A. (2010), *Elias Bickerman as a Historian of the Jews*, Tübingen: Mohr Siebeck.

Beard, M. (2019), 'Remembering Fergus Millar: How to Disagree', *Times Literary Supplement Blog*. Available at: https://www.the-tls.co.uk/articles/ remembering-fergus-millar-disagree/ (accessed 28 June 2021).

Benjamin, W. (1997), 'The Translator's Task', trans. S. Rendall, *Traduction, Terminologie, Rédaction*, 10 (2): 151–65.

Bentley, J. (1983), *Humanist and Holy Writ: New Testament Scholarship in the Renaissance*, Princeton, NJ: Princeton University Press.

Bhabha, H. K. (1990), *Nation and Narration*, London and New York: Routledge.

Bhabha, H. K. (2021), 'Hospitality and Psychiatry: Just a Gut Feeling', in L. Laubscher, D. Hook and M. U. Desai (eds), *Fanon, Phenomenology, and Psychology*, London: Routledge.

Bialas, W. and A. Rabinbach, eds (2007), *Nazi Germany and the Humanities*, London: Oneworld Publications.

Billings, J. and M. Leonard, eds (2015), *Tragedy and the Idea of Modernity*, Oxford: Oxford University Press.

Bollack, J. (1998), *Jacob Bernays: un homme entre deux mondes*, Lille: Presse universitaires Septentrion.

Bousfield, C. (1890), *English Verse Translated into Latin Verse, Chiefly Elegiacs*, London: Nabu Press.

Bowersock, G. (1991), 'Momigliano's Quest for the Person', *History and Theory*, 30: 27–36.

Boyarin, D. (2015), *A Travelling Homeland: The Babylonian Talmud as Diaspora*, Philadelphia, PA: University of Pennsylvania Press.

Boyarin, D. (2018), *Judaism: The Genealogy of a Modern Notion*, New Brunswick, NJ: Rutgers University Press.

Brady, S. (2005), *Masculinity and Male Homosexuality in Britain*, Houndsmills: Palgrave Macmillan.

Brennan, T. (1992), *Interpretations of the Flesh: Freud and Femininity*, London: Routledge.

Brennan, T. (2004), *The Transmission of Affect*, Ithaca, NY: Cornell University Press.

Brett, R., Viscount Esher (1923) *Ionicus*, London: J. Murray.

Bridenbaugh, C. (1963), 'The Great Mutation', *American Historical Review*, 68: 315–31.

Briggs, W. Jr (2002), '"Second-Hand Superiority": Basil Lanneau Gildersleeve and the English', *Polis*, 19: 109–23.

Briggs, W. W. and W. M. Calder, eds (1990), *Classical Scholarship: A Biographical Encyclopedia*, New York: Garland Publishing.

Brodkin, K. (1998), *How Jews became White Folk and What that Says about Race in America*, New Brunswick, NJ: Rutgers University Press.

Broughton, T. (1999), *Men of Letters, Writing Lives: Masculinity and Literary Autobiography in the Late Victorian Period*, London: Routledge.

Brown, D. (2008), *Richard Hofstadter: An Intellectual Biography*, Chicago, IL: University of Chicago Press.

Brown, P. (1988), 'Arnaldo Dante Momigliano, 1908–1987', *Proceedings of the British Academy*, 74: 405–42.

Bullard, P. and A. Tadié, eds (2016), *Ancients and Moderns in Europe: Comparative Perspectives*, Oxford: Oxford University Press.

Butler, J. (1999), *Gender Trouble: Feminism and the Subversion of Identity*, New York: Routledge.

Butler, J. (2002), *Antigone's Claim*, New York: Columbia University Press.

Butler, J. R. M. (1925), *Henry Montagu Butler: Master of Trinity College, Cambridge 1886–1918*, London and New York: Longmans, Green.

Calder, W. M. (1990), 'Werner Jaeger', in W. W. Briggs and W. M. Calder III (eds), *Classical Scholarship: A Biographical Encyclopedia*, 211–26, New York and London: Garland.

Calder, W. M. (1992), 'The Refugee Classical Scholars in the USA: An Evaluation of their Contribution', *Illinois Classical Studies*, 17: 153–73.

Calder, W. M., ed. (1992), *Werner Jaeger Reconsidered: Proceedings of the Second Oldfather Conference Held on the Campus of the University of Illinois at Urbana-Champaign, April 26–28, 1990, Illinois Classical Studies Supplement* 3, Atlanta, GA: Scholars Press.

Calder, W. and M. Braun (1996), '"Tell it Hitler! Ecco!" Paul Friedländer on Werner Jaeger's *Paideia*', *Quaderni di storia*, 43: 211–48.

Capettini E. and Rabinowitz, N., eds (2021) *Classics and Prison Education*, New York and London: Routledge.

Carter, J. (1949), 'A Hand-List of the Printed Works of William Johnson, afterwards Cory: Fellow of King's College, Cambridge and an Assistant Master at Eton', *Transactions of the Cambridge Bibliographical Society*, 1: 69–87.

Caulfield, J. (2013), *Overcoming Matthew Arnold: Ethics in Culture and Criticism*, Farnham: Ashgate.

Cavell, S. (1994), *The Pitch of Philosophy: Autobiographical Exercises*, Cambridge, MA: Harvard University Press.

Chakrabarty, D. (2000), *Provincializing Europe: Postcolonial Thought and Historical Difference*, Princeton, NJ: Princeton University Press.

Chandler, J. (2013), *The Archaeology of Sympathy*, Chicago, IL: University of Chicago Presss.

Chopp, R. (2010), 'Martin Ostwald (1922–2010)', April 12. Available at: https://www.swarthmore.edu/profile/martin-ostwald-1922-2010 (accessed 30 June 2021).

Clemente, G. (2009), 'Pagani, Ebrei, Cristiani nella riflessione storica di Arnaldo Momigliano', *Rivista Storica Italiana*, 129: 626–38.

Collini, S. (1994), *Matthew Arnold: A Critical Portrait*, Oxford: Clarendon Press.

Collins, P. H. ([1990] 2000), *Black Feminist Thought: Knowledge, Consciousness and the Politics of Empowerment*, London and New York: Routledge.

Collins, P. H. (2019), *Intersectionality as Critical Social Theory*, Durham, NC: Duke University Press.

Compton Mackenzie, F. (1950), *William Cory: A Biography*, London: Constable.

Connell, W. (1950), *The Educational Thought and Influence of Matthew Arnold*, London: Routledge.

Conybeare, C. and S. Goldhill, (2020), *Classical Philology and Theology: Disavowal, Entanglement and the God-Like Scholar*, Cambridge: Cambridge University Press.

Cook J. (2019), '"Hear and Shudder!": John Chrysostom's Therapy of the Soul', in C. de Wet and W. Mayer (eds), *Revisioning John Chrysostom: New Approaches, New Perspectives*, 247–75, Leiden: Brill.

Cooper, D. (2015), *Everyday Utopias: The Conceptual Life of Promising Spaces*, Durham, NC, and London: Duke University Press.

Cooper, D. (2013), *Everyday Utopias: The Conceptual Life of Promising Spaces*, Durham, NC: Duke University Press.

Cooper, E. (2009), *Vinnie Ream: An American Sculptor*, Chicago, IL: University of Chicago Press.

Cory, W. (1858), *Ionica*, London: Smith, Elder and Co. .

Cory, W. (1871), *Lucretilis: An Introduction to the Art of Writing Latin Lyric Verses*, Eton and London: E. P. Williams and Son.

Cory, W. (1873), *Iophon: An Introduction to the Art of Writing Greek Iambic Verses*, Eton and London: E. P. Williams and Son.

Coser, L. (1984), *Refugee Scholars in America: Their Impact and Their Experiences*, New Haven, CT: Yale University Press.

Crawford, S., K. Ulmschneider and J. Elsner, eds (2017), *The Ark of Civilization*, Oxford: Oxford University Press.

Darwish, M. (2011), *If I Were Another*, trans. F. Joudah, New York: Fsg Adult.

Daston, L. and G. Most (2015), 'History of Science and History of Philologies', *Isis*, 106: 378–90.

de Wet, C. (2019), 'The Preacher's Diet: Gluttony, Regimen and Psycho-Somatic Health in the Thought of John Chrysostom', in C. de Wet and W. Mayer (eds), *Revisioning John Chrysostom: New Approaches, New Perspectives*, 410–63, Leiden: Brill.

de Wet, C. and W. Mayer, eds (2019), *Revisioning John Chrysostom: New Approaches, New Perspectives*, Leiden: Brill.

DeLaura, D. J. (1969), *Hebrew and Hellene in Victorian Britain*, Austin, TX: University of Texas Press.

Delacroix, C., F. Dosse and P. Garcia (2004), *Histoire et historiens en France depuis 1945*, Paris: Association pour la diffusion de la pensée française.

Deutsch, Monroe E. (1941), *Our Legacy of Religious Freedom*, New York: National Conference of Christians and Jews.

Diggle, J., ed. (2021), *The Cambridge Greek Lexicon*, Cambridge: Cambridge University Press.

Dixon, T. (2017), *Weeping Britannia: Portrait of a Nation in Tears*, Oxford: Oxford University Press.

Dosse, F. (2020), *Pierre Vidal-Naquet*, Paris: Éditions La Découverte.

Dowling. L. (1994), *Hellenism and Homosexuality in Victorian Oxford*, Ithaca, NY: Cornell University Press.

Drake, S. (2013), *Slandering the Jew: Sexuality and Difference in Early Christian Texts*, Philadelphia, PA: University of Pennsylvania Press.

Dunkelgrun, T. (2020), 'The Philology of Judaism: Zacharias Frankel, the Septuagint and the Jewish Study of Ancient Greek in the Nineteenth Century', in C. Conybeare and S. Goldhill (eds), *Classical Philology and Theology: Entanglement, Disavowal, and the Godlike Scholar*, 63–85, Cambridge: Cambridge University Press.

Dunkle, B. (2016), *Enchantment and Creed in the Hymns of Ambrose of Milan*, Oxford: Oxford University Press.

Dunn, G. and W. Mayer, eds (2015), *Christians Shaping Identity from the Roman Empire to Byzantium: Studies Inspired by Pauline Allen, Vigiliae Christianae Supplements*, 132, Leiden: Brill.

Eddo-Lodge, R. (2017), *Why I'm No Longer Talking to White People about Race*, London: Bloomsbury Publishing.

Elder, O. and A. Mullen (2019), *The Language of Roman Letters: Bilingual Epistolography from Cicero to Fronto*, Cambridge: Cambridge University Press.

Elsner, J. (2013), 'Paideia: Ancient Concept and Modern Reception', *International Journal of Classical Reception*, 20: 136–52.

Elsner, J. (2017), 'Pfeiffer, Fraenkel, and Refugee Scholarship in Oxford during and after the Second World War', in S. Crawford, K. Ulmschneider and J. Elsner (eds), *Ark of Civilization: Refugee Scholars and Oxford University*, 25–49, Oxford: Oxford University Press.

Elsner, J. (2021), 'Room with a Few: Eduard Fraenkel and the Receptions of Reception', in S. Pelling and C. Harrison (eds), *Classical Scholarship and Its History: From the Renaissance to the* Present, 317–45, Berlin: De Gruyter.

Eribon, D. (2013), *Returning to Reims*, trans. M. Lucey, London: Allen Lane.

Eshelman, S. (2012), *The Social World of Intellectuals in the Roman Empire*, Cambridge: Cambridge University Press.

Evangelista, S. (2010), 'Swinburne's Galleries', *The Yearbook of English Studies*, 40: 160–79.

Fanon, F. ([1952] 2008), *Black Skin, White Masks*, trans. C. Markmann, New York: Grove Weidenfeld.

Fanon, F. ([1961] 2004), *The Wretched of the Earth*, trans. R. Philcox, New York: Grove Press.

Farrar, F. W., ed. (1867), *Essays on a Liberal Education*, London: McMillan's.

Feeney, D. (2016), *Beyond Greek: The Beginnings of Latin Literature*, Cambridge, MA: Harvard University Press.

Felman, S. and D. Laub (1992), *Testimony: Crises of Witnessing in Literature, Psychoanalysis and History*, New York and London: Routledge.

Felski, R. (2020), *Hooked: Art and Attachment*, Chicago, IL: University of Chicago Press.

Felski, R. (2021), 'Recognizing Class', *New Literary History*, 52: 95–117.

Field, G. (1981), *Evangelist of Race: The Germanic Vision of Houston Stuart Chamberlain*, New York: Columbia University Press.

Finkman, S., A. Behrendt and A. Walter, eds (2018), *Antike Erzähl- und Deutungsmuster: zwischen Exemplarität und Transformation*, Berlin: De Gruyter.

Fleming, K. (2006), 'The Use and Abuse of Antiquity: The Politics and Morality of Appropriation', in Martindale and Thomas (eds), 127–37, Malden, MA, and Oxford: Blackwell's.

François, W. (2016), *Vernacular Bible and Religious Reform in the Middle Ages and Early Modern Era*, Leuven: Peeters.

Frederiksen, P. (2008), *Augustine and the Jews: A Christian Defence of Jews and Judaism*, New York: Doubleday.

Frederiksen, P. (2018), 'How Jewish is God? Divine Ethnicity in Paul's Theology', *Journal of Biblical Literature*, 137 (1): 193–212.

Frederiksen, P. and O. Ishai (2006), 'Christian Anti-Judaism: Polemics and Policies', in S. T. Katz (ed.), *The Cambridge History of Judaism*, Vol. 4: *The Late Roman-Rabbinic Period*, 977–1034, Cambridge: Cambridge University Press.

Frederiksen, P., M. Thiesen, J. Eyl, B. Nongbri, T. Engberg-Pedersen and E. Barreto (2020), 'Symposium: Paul'. Available at: https://syndicate.network/symposia/theology/paul-the-pagans-apostle/ (2 August 2021).

Gager, J. (1983), *The Origins of Anti-Semitism: Attitudes towards Judaism in Pagan and Christian Antiquity*, Princeton, NJ: Princeton University Press.

Gagnier, R. (1991), *Subjectivities: A History of Self-Representation in Britain, 1832–1920*, Oxford: Oxford University Press.

Gallop, J. (1985), *Reading Lacan*, London and Ithaca, NY: Cornell University Press.

Gallop, J. (1988), *Thinking through the Body*, New York: Columbia University Press.

Gallop, J. (1997), *Feminist Accused of Sexual Harassment*, Durham, NC: Duke University Press.

Gange, D. (2009), 'Odysseus in Eden: Gladstone's Homer and the Idea of Universal Epic, 1850–1880', *Journal of Victorian Culture*, 14 (2): 190–206.

Garnsey, P. (2016), 'Finley and Other Scholars: The Case of Finley and Momigliano', in D. Jew, R. Osborne and M. Scott (eds), *M. I. Finley: An Ancient Historian and His Impact*, 193–209, Cambridge: Cambridge University Press.

Gelhaus, H. (1989), *Der Streit um Luthers Bibelverdeutschung im 16. Und 17. Jahrhundert* 2 voll, Tübingen: Max Niemeyer Verlag.

Gentzler, E. (1993), *Contemporary Translation Theories*, London and New York: Routledge.

Gibson, R. K. and C. L. Whitton, eds (forthcoming), *Cambridge Critical Guide to Latin Literature*, Cambridge: Cambridge University Press.

Gildersleeve, B. (1930), *Selections from the Brief Mention of Basil Lanneau Gildersleeve*, ed. C. Miller, Baltimore, MD: Johns Hopkins Press.

Gildersleeve, B. (1992), *The Selected Classical Papers of Basil Gildersleeve*, ed. W. Briggs Jr, Atlanta, GA: Scholars' Press/American Philological Association.

Gilman, S. (1985), *Difference and Pathology: Stereotypes of Sexuality, Race and Madness*, Ithaca, NY: .Cornell University Press

Gilman, S. (1991), *The Jew's Body*, New York and London: Routledge.

Gilroy, P. (1987), *There Ain't No Black in the Union Jack*, London and New York: Routledge.

Gilroy, P. (1993), *The Black Atlantic: Modernity and Double Consciousness*, New York and London: Verso.

Glaude, E. (2021), *Begin Again: James Baldwin's America and Its Urgent Lessons for Today*, London: Chatto and Windus.

Goldberg, S., S. Ury and K. Weiser (2021), *Key Concepts in the Study of Antisemitism*, London: Palgrave Macmillan.

Goldhill, S. (2002), *Who Needs Greek? Contests in the Cultural History of Hellenism*, Cambridge: Cambridge University Press.

Goldhill, S. (2008), *Jerusalem, City of Longing*, Cambridge, MA: Harvard University Press.

Goldhill, S. (2011), *Victorian Culture and Classical Antiquity: Art, Opera, Fiction and the Proclamation of Modernity*, Princeton, NJ: Princeton University Press.

Goldhill, S. (2013), *Sophocles and the Language of Tragedy*, Oxford: Oxford University Press.

Goldhill, S. (2015), *The Buried Life of Things: How Objects Made History in Nineteenth-Century Britain*, Cambridge; Cambridge University Press.

Goldhill, S. (2016a), 'Polytheism and Tragedy' in E. Eidinow, J. Kindt and R. Osborne (eds), *Theologies of Ancient Greek* Religion, 153–75, Cambridge: Cambridge University Press.

Goldhill, S. (2016b), *A Very Queer Family Indeed: Sex, Religion and the Bensons in Victorian Literature*, Chicago, IL: University of Chicago Press.

Goldhill, S. (2020), *Preposterous Poetics: The Politics and Aesthetics of Form in Late Antiquity*, Cambridge: Cambridge University Press.

Goldhill, S. (forthcoming a), *The Christian Invention of Time: Temporality and the Literature of Late Antiquity*, Cambridge: Cambridge University Press.

Goldhill, S. (forthcoming b), 'Latin Literature on Greek', in R. K. Gibson and C. L. Whitton (eds), *The Cambridge Critical Guide to Latin Literature*, Cambridge: Cambridge University Press.

Goldhill, S., ed. (2020), *Being Urban: Community, Conflict and Belonging in the Middle East*, London: Routledge.

Goldman, E. (1917), *Anarchism and Other Essays*, New York: Mother Earth Publishing.

Goldstein, E. (2006), *The Price of Whiteness: Jews, Race and American Identity*, Princeton, NJ: Princeton University Press.

Gordon, J. (2015), 'What Blacks Should Think when Jews Choose Whiteness? An Ode to Baldwin', *Critical Philosophy of Race*, 3: 22758.

Grafton, A. (1998), Jacob Bernays, Joseph Scaliger and Others', in D. N. Myers and D. B. Ruderman (eds), *The Jewish Past Revisited: Reflections on Modern Jewish Historians*, 17–38, New Haven, CT: Yale University Press.

Grafton, A. (2007), 'Momigliano's Method and the Warburg Institute: Studies in His Middle Period', in P. N. Miller (ed.), *Momigliano and Antiquarianism: Foundations of the Modern Cultural* Sciences, 97–126, Toronto: Toronto University Press.

Grafton, A. (2020), 'Tell Me a Story', *Tablet*, 1 September 2020. Available at: https://www.tabletmag.com/sections/arts-letters/articles/arnaldo-momigliano-anthony-grafton (accessed 19 October 2021).

Grafton, A. and J. Weinberg (2011), '*I Have Always Loved the Holy Tongue*': Isaac Casaubon, the Jews and a Forgotten Chapter in Renaissance Scholarship, Cambridge, MA: Harvard University Press.

Graham, E. (1920), *The Harrow Life of Henry Montagu Butler, D.D.*, London: Longmans, Green.

Greatrex, G. and H. Elton, eds (2015), *Shifting Genres in Late Antiquity*, Farnham: Ashgate.

Grossman, D. ([1986, 1989] 2010), *See Under: Love*, London: Vintage.

Gruen, E. (1998), *Heritage and Hellenism: The Reinvention of Jewish Tradition*, Berkeley, CA: University of California Press.

Gruen, E. (2002), *Diaspora: Jews amidst Greeks and Romans*, Cambridge, MA: Harvard University Press.

Gruen, E. (2008), 'The *Letter of Aristeas* and the Cultural Context of the Septuagint', in M. Karrer and W. Kraus (eds), *Translating the Septuagint for Ptolemy's Library: Myth and History*, 134–56, Tübingen: Mohr Siebeck.

Gruen, E. (2010), *Rethinking the Other in Antiquity*, Princeton, NJ: Princeton University Press.

Gruen, E. (2018), 'Wandering Jew', *Ancient Jew Review*, 12 September. Available at: https://www.ancientjewreview.com/articles/2018/9/12/a-wandering-jew-some-reflections?rq=Gruen (accessed 9 July 2021).

Guglielmo, T. (2003), *White on Arrival: Italians, Race, Color and Power in Chicago, 1890–1945*, New York and Oxford: Oxford University Press.

Güthenke, C. (2020), *Feeling and Classical Philology: Knowing Antiquity in German Scholarship, 1770–1920*, Cambridge: Cambridge University Press.

Haley, S. (2009), 'Be Not Afraid of the Dark: Critical Race Theories and Classical Studies', in L. Nasrallah and E. Schüssler Fiorenza (eds), *Prejudice and Christian Beginnings: Investigating Racism, Gender, and Ethnicity in Early Christian Studies*, 27–50, Minneapolis, MN: Fortress Press.

Hall, C. (2012), *Macaulay and Son: Architects of Imperial Britain*, New Haven, CT: Yale University Press.

Hall, E. (1995), 'Lawcourt Dramas: The Power of Performance in Greek Forensic Oratory', *Bulletin of the Institute of Classical Studies*, 40 (1): 39–58.

Hall, E. and H. Stead (2020), *A People's History of Classics: Class and Greco-Roman Antiquity in Britain and Ireland 1689–1939*, London: Routledge.

Hallett, J. (2018), 'The Endeavours and *Exempla* of the German Refugee Classicists, Eva Lehmann Fiesel and Ruth Fiesel', in S. Finkman, A. Behrendt and A. Walter (eds), *Antike Erzähl- und Deutungsmuster: Zwischen Exemplarität und Transformation. Ancient Paradigms of Narrative and Interpretation: Between Exemplarity and Transformation*, 655–93, Berlin and New York: De Gruyter.

Hallett, J. (2019), 'Expanding Our Professional Embrace: The American Philological Society/Society for Classical Studies, 1970–2019', *The American Philological Association*, 149: 61–87.

Hallett, J. P. and T. Van Nortwick, eds (1997), *Compromising Traditions: The Personal Voice in Classical Scholarship*, London and New York: Routledge.

Hammerschlag, S. (2010), *The Figural Jew: Politics and Identity in Post-War French Thought*, Chicago, IL: University of Chicago Press.

Hammerschlag, S. (2016), *Broken Tablets: Levinas, Derrida and the Literary Afterlife of Religion*, New York: Columbia University Press.

Häntzschel, H. (2001), 'Profesionell ohne Profession: Arbeitsfelder von Philoginnen jüdischer Herkunft', in W. Barner and C. König (eds), *Zeitenwechsel; germanistische Literaturwissenschaft vor und nach 1945*, 65–73, Frankfurt: Fischer Taschenbuch Verlag.

Haraway, D. (1988), 'Situated Knowledges: The Science Question in Feminism and the Privilege of Partial Perspectives', *Feminist Studies*, 14: 575–99.

Harford, F. K. (1890), *Epigrammatica Serious, Semi-serious and Divertive*, London: Henry Sotheran.

Harloe, K., N. Momigliano and A. Farnoux, eds (2018), *Hellenomania*, Abingdon: Routledge.

Harris, W. (2017), 'Badien, Ernst, 1925–2011', *Biographical Memoirs of Fellows of the British Academy*, 16: 1–17.

Harris, W., ed. (2013), *Moses Finley and Politics*, Leiden: Brill.

Harrison, C. (2000), *Augustine: Christian Truth and Fractured Humanity*, Oxford: Oxford University Press.

Hart, J. M. (1892), 'Aims and Methods of the Courses in Rhetoric and in English Philology', *Cornell Magazine*, 4 (8): 276–83.

Hartman, S. (2019), *Wayward Lives, Beautiful Experiments*, New York: W. W. Norton.

Hartog, F. (2007), *Vidal-Naquet: Historien en personne: L'Homme-mémoire et le moment-mémoire*, Paris: La Découverte.

Hartog, F. (2017), *La Nation, la religion, l'avenir: Sur les Traces d'Ernest Renan*, Paris: Gallimard.

Hartog, F., P. Schmitt-Pantel and A. Schnapp, eds (1998), *Pierre Vidal-Naquet: Un Historien dans la cité*, Paris: La Découverte.

Haynes, N. (2019), *A Thousand Ships*, London: Mantle.

Hentoff, N. (1969), 'Introduction', in *Black Anti-Semitism and Jewish Racism*, J. Baldwin, E. Raab, J. Kaufman, A. W. Miller, W. H. Booth, W. Karp, H. R. Shapiro, H. Cruse, A. Vorspan and J. Lester, New York: E. P. Dutton, originally published in the *New York Times*, 19 April 1967.

Heschel, S. (2008), *The Aryan Jesus: Christian Theologians and the Bible in Nazi Germany*, Princeton, NJ: Princeton University Press.

Highet, G. (1949), *The Classical Tradition: Greek and Roman Influences on Western Literature*, Oxford: Oxford University Press.

Honig, B. (2021), *A Feminist Theory of Refusal*, Cambridge, MA: Harvard University Press.

Honigman, S. (2007), 'The Narrative Function of the King and the Library in the Letter of Aristeas', in T. Rajak (ed.), *Jewish Perspectives on Hellenistic Rulers*, 128–46, Berkeley, CA: University of California Press.

hooks, bell, (1981), *Ain't I a Woman? Black Women and Feminism*, Boston, MA: South End Press.

Horkheimer, M. and T. Adorno ([1947] 2002), *Dialectic of Enlightenment: Philosophical Frgaments*, ed. G. Noerr, trans. E. Jephcott, Stanford, CA: Stanford University Press.

Horsfall, N. (1990), 'Eduard Fraenkel', in Briggs and Calder (eds), *Classical Scholarship: A Biographical Encyclopedia*, 61–7, New York: Garland Publishing.

Howard, T. A. L. (2009), *Religion and the Rise of Historicism: W.M.L. de Wette, Jacob Burckhardt, and the Theological Origins of Nineteenth-Century Historical Consciousness*, Cambridge: Cambridge University Press.

Idel, M. (2007), 'Arnaldo Momigliano and Gershom Sholem on Jewish History and Tradition', in P. N. Miller (ed.), *Momigliano and Antiquarianism: Foundations of the Modern Cultural* Sciences, 312–33, Toronto: Toronto University Press.

Ignatiev, N. (1995), *How the Irish became White*, New York and London: Routledge.

Isaac, B. (2004), *The Invention of Racism in Antiquity*, Princeton, NJ: Princeton University Press.

Jameson, F. (1981), *The Political Unconscious: Narrative as a Socially Symbolic Act*, London and New York: Cornell University Press.

Jardine, L. (1993), *Erasmus Man of Letters: The Construction of Charisma in Print*, Princeton, NJ: Princeton University Press.

Jew, D., R. Osborne and M. Scott, eds (2016), *M. I. Finley: An Ancient Historian and His Impact*, Cambridge: Cambridge University Press.

Jocelyn, H. (1994), 'Charles Oscar Brink, 1907–1994', *Proceedings of the British Academy*, 97: 319–54.

Jones, H. M. (1974), *Revolution and Romanticism*, Cambridge, MA: Harvard University Press.

Kallendorf, C. W. (2010), 'Introduction', in C. W. Kallendorf (ed.), *A Companion to the Classical Tradition*, 1–4, Oxford: Wiley-Blackwell.

Kallendorf, C., ed. (2010), *A Companion to the Classical Tradition*, Oxford: Wiley-Blackwell.

Kaplan, M. (2005), *Sodom on the Thames: Sex, Love and Scandal in Wilde Times*, Ithaca, NY: Cornell University Press.

Karabel, J. (2005), *The Chosen: The Hidden History of Exclusion at Harvard, Yale and Princeton*, Boston, MA: Houghton Mifflin Harcourt.

Katz, S. T., ed. (2006), *The Cambridge History of Judaism*, Vol. 4: *The Late Roman-Rabbinic Period*, Cambridge: Cambridge University Press.

Kelly, J. N. D. (1985), 'Review of R. L. Wilken, *John Chrysostom and the Jews: Rhetoric and Reality in the Late 4th Century* (Eugene, OR: Wipf & Stock, 1983)', *Journal of Theological Studies*, 36 (2): 483–4.

Kennedy, R. F., C. S. Roy and M. Goldman (2013), *Race and Ethnicity in the Classical World: An Anthology of Primary Sources in Translation*, Indianapolis, IN, and Cambridge, MA: Hackett.

Kenney, E. J. (1977), Review, 'M. Hellewell, *A Book of Topical Latin Verse*, Part 2, Sowerby Bridge, West Yorkshire, published by the author', *Classical Review*, 27 (2): 328.

Kindt, J. and R. Osborne, eds (2016), *Theologies of Ancient Greek Religion*, Cambridge: Cambridge University Press.

Klingenstein, S. (1991), *Jews in the American Academy 1900–1940: The Dynamics of Intellectual Assimilation*, New Haven, CT: Yale University Press.

Knausgaard, K.-O. (2012–18), *My Struggle*, 6 vols, trans. D. Bartlett, Harmondsworth: Penguin.

König, C. and Thouard, D., eds (2010), *La Philologie au présent: Pour Jean Bollack*, Villeneuve-d'Ascq: Presse universitaires du Septentrion.

Konig, J. and N. Wiater, eds (forthcoming), *Late Hellenistic Greek Literature in Dialogue*, Cambridge: Cambridge University Press.

Kraemer, J. L. (1999), 'The Death of an Orientalist: Paul Kraus from Prague to Cairo', in M. Kramer (ed.), *The Jewish Discovery of Islam: Studies in Honour of Bernard Lewis*, 181–223, Tel Aviv: Moshe Dayan Center for Middle Eastern Studies.

Kramer, M., ed. (1999), *The Jewish Discovery of Islam: Studies in Honour of Bernard Lewis*, Tel Aviv: Moshe Dayan Center for Middle Eastern Studies.

Kurtz, P. (2021), 'The Philological Apparatus: Science, Text and Nation in the Nineteenth Century', *Critical Inquiry*, 47: 747–76.

Laborde, C. (2017), *Liberalism's Religion*, Cambridge, MA: Harvard University Press.

Larsen, T. (2014), *The Slain God: Anthropologists and the Christian Faith*, Oxford: Oxford University Press.

Laubscher, L., D. Hook and M. Desai, eds (2021), *Fanon, Phenomenology and Psychiatry*, New York and London: Routledge.

Leonard, M. (2005), *Athens in Paris: Ancient Greek Thought and the Political in Post-War French Thought*, Oxford: Oxford University Press.

Leonard, M. (2012), *Socrates and the Jews: Hellenism and Hebraism from Moses Mendelssohn to Sigmund Freud*, Chicago, IL: University of Chicago Press.

Levine, M. M. (1985), 'Annals of an Orthodox Jew at Wellesley in the '60s', *Wellesley Alumnae Magazine*, 70: 14–16.

Levine, M. M. (2018), 'Iphigenia in Jerusalem: Sacrifice and Survival in Greek
    and Jewish Culture', *Eidolon*, 22 March 2018. Available at: https://eidolon.
    pub/iphigenia-in-jerusalem-48ba4f15565f (accessed 3 July 2020).

Limor, O. and G. Stroumsa, eds (1996), *Contra Iudaeos: Ancient and Medieval
    Polemics between Christians and Jews*, Tübingen: J. C. B. Mohr (Paul Siebeck).

Lockhart, J. G. (1850), 'Review of *A Critical History of the Language and
    Literature of Ancient Greece* by William Mure of Caldwell', *Quarterly Review*,
    87: 434–68.

Losemann, V. (1977), *Nationalsozialismus und Antike: Studien zur Entwicklung
    des Faches Alte Geschichte 1933–1945*, Hamburg: Hoffmann und Campe.

Losemann, V. (2006), 'Classics in the Second World War', in A. Bialas and
    W. Rabinbach (eds), *Nazi Germany and the Humanities*, 306–39, Oxford:
    Oneworld.

Louis, M. (2005), 'Gods and Mysteries: The Revival of Paganism and the
    Remaking of Mythography through the Nineteenth Century', *Victorian
    Studies*, 47: 329–61.

Loyer, E. ([2015] 2018), *Lévi-Strauss: A Biography*, trans. N. Vinsonneau and
    J. Magidoff, Cambridge: Polity Press.

Lyttelton, E. (1897), *Are We to Go on with Latin Verses?*, London: Longmans,
    Green.

Lyttelton, Lord and W. E. Gladstone (1861), *Translations*, London: Bernard
    Quaritch.

MacDonald, G. (2016), *Biblical Criticism in Early Modern Europe: Erasmus, the
    Johannine Comma and Trinitarian Debate*, Leiden: Brill.

MacDonald, M. (2007), '"A Man Most Awesome and Most Gentle": In
    Memoriam Thomas Rosenmeyer (3 April 1920–6 February 2007)', *Arion*, 15:
    19–28.

MacSweeney, N. et al. (2019), 'Claiming the Classical: The Greco-Roman World
    in Contemporary Political Discourse', *Bulletin of the Council of University
    Classical Departments*, 48: 1–19.

Mahmood, S. (2015), *Religious Difference in a Secular Age: A Minority Report*,
    Princeton, NJ: Princeton University Press.

Mandler, P. (2016), 'Educating the Nation III: Social Mobility', *Transactions of the
    Royal Historical Society*, 26: 1–23.

Manning, J. G., ed. (2010), *Writing History in the Time of War:. Michael
    Rostovtzeff, Elias Bickerman and the 'Hellenization of Asia'*, Stuttgart: Franz
    Steiner.

Marcus, L. (1994), *Auto/biographical Discourses*, Manchester: Manchester
    University Press.

Martindale, C. (1995), 'Ruins of Rome: T. S. Eliot and the Presence of the Past',
    Arion, 3: 109–40.

Martindale, C. and R. Thomas, eds (2006), *Classics and the Uses of Reception*, Oxford: Blackwell Publishing.

Mayer, W. (2015a), 'Shaping the Sick Soul: Reshaping the Identity of John Chrysostom', in G. Dunn and W. Mayer (eds), *Christians Shaping Identity from the Roman Empire to Byzantium: Studies Inspired by Pauline Allen, Vigiliae Christianae Supplements*, 140–64, Leiden: Brill.

Mayer, W. (2015b), 'Medicine in Transition: Christian Adaptation in the Later Fourth-Century East', in G. Greateix and H. Elton (eds), *Shifting Genres in Late Antiquity*, 11–26, Farnham: Ashgate.

Mayer, W. (2019), 'Preaching Hatred? John Chrysostom, Neuroscience and the Jews', in C. de Wet and W. Mayer (eds), *Revisioning John Chrysostom: New Approaches, New Perspectives*, 58–136, Leiden: Brill.

McClintock, A. (1995), *Imperial Leather: Race, Gender and Sexuality in the Colonial Context*, New York: Routledge.

McCoskey, D. (2012), *Race: Antiquity and Its Legacy*, London: Bloomsbury Publishing.

McCoskey, D., ed. (2021), *The Cultural History of Race, Volume One: A Cultural History of Race in Antiquity (500 BCE–800 CE)*, London: Bloomsbury.

McLennan, R. (1990), *Early Christian Texts on Jews and Judaism*, Atlanta, GA: Scholars' Press.

Meckler, M., ed. (2006), *Classical Antiquity and the Politics of America*, Waco, TX: Baylor University Press.

Mendelsohn, D. (1999), *The Elusive Embrace: Desire and the Riddle of Identity*, New York: A. Knopf.

Mendelsohn, D. (2006), *The Lost: A Search for Six of the Six Million*, New York: HarperCollins.

Mendelsohn, D. (2017), *An Odyssey: A Father, a Son and an Epic*, New York: William Collins.

Mendelsohn, D. (2020), *Three Rings: A Tale of Exile, Narrative and Fate*, Charlottesville, VA, and London: University of Virginia Press.

Miller, M. (2011), *The Song of Achilles*, London: HarperCollins.

Miller, M. (2018), *Circe*, New York: Bloomsbury Publishing.

Miller, P., ed. (2007), *Momigliano and Antiquarianism*, Toronto: University of Toronto Press.

Moi, T. (1999), *'What is a Woman?' and Other Essays*, Oxford: Oxford University Press.

Molina, N. (2014), *How Race is Made in America: Immigration, Citizenship, and the Historical Power of Racial Scripts*, Berkeley, CA: Univerrsity of California Press.

Momigliano, A. (1971), 'Eduard Fraenkel', *Encounter*, 36 (2): 55–6.

Momigliano, A. (1974), 'Jews in Classical Scholarship', *Encyclopaedia Judaica Handbook*, 225–7.

Momigliano, A. (1994a), 'J. G. Droysen: Between Greeks and Jews', in G. W. Bowersock and T. J. Cornell (eds), *A. D. Momigliano: Studies on Modern Scholarship*, 147–61, Berkeley, CA: University of California Press.

Momigliano, A. (1994b), *Essays on Ancient and Modern Judaism*, ed. S. Berti, trans. M. Masella-Gayley, Chicago, IL: University of Chicago Press.

Montagu Butler, H. (1887), 'Henry Martyn: A Sermon Preached in Trinity Church, Cambridge, October 17th, 1887', Sermon, Cambridge, n.p.

Montagu Butler, H. (1896), 'An Attempt to Render Psalm cvii in Latin Elegiac Verse', n.p. [Cambridge].

Montagu Butler, H. (1913), 'Some Remarks on the Teaching of Greek and Latin Verses and on the Value of Translations from the Classics', London: reprint from *Classical Association Proceedings 1913*.

Montagu Butler, H. (1914), *Some Leisure Hours of a Long Life: Translations into Greek, Latin and English Verse, from 1850–1914*, Cambridge: Bowes & Bowes.

Myers, D. (2002), *Resisting History: Historicism and Its Discontents in German Jewish Thought*, Princeton, NJ: Princeton University Press.

Myers, D., and D. Ruderman, eds (1998), *The Jewish Past Revisited: Reflections on Modern Jewish Historians*, New Haven, CT: Yale University Press.

Näf, B. (1986), *Von Perikles zu Hitler? Die athenische Demokratie und die deutsche Althistorie bis 1945*, New York: P. Lang.

Näf, B. and T. Kammasch, eds (2001), *Antike und Altertumswissenschaft in der Zeit von Faschismus und Nationalsozialismus, Kolloquium Universität Zürich 14–17 Oktober 1998*, Mandelbachtal and Cambridge. Edition Cicero.

Nasrallah, L. and E. Schlüsser Fiorenza, eds (2009), *Prejudice and Christian Beginnings: Investigating Race, Gender and Ethnicity in Early Christian Studies*, Minneapolis, MN: Fortress Press.

Nelson, D. (2017), *Tough Enough: Arbus, Arendt, Didion, McCarthy, Sontag, Weil*, Chicago, IL: University of Chicago Press.

Niehoff, M. (2001), *Philo on Jewish Identity and Culture*, Tübingen: Mohr Siebeck.

Niehoff, M. (2018), *Philo of Alexandria: An Intellectual Biography*, New Haven, CT: Yale University Press.

Nirenberg, D. (2013), *Anti-Judaism: The Western Tradition*, New York: W. W. Norton.

Nisbet, G. (2013), *Greek Epigram in Reception: J. A. Symonds, Oscar Wilde, and the Invention of Desire, 1805–1929*, Oxford: Oxford University Press.

Nongbri, B. (2013), *Before Religion: A History of a Modern Concept*, New Haven, CT: Yale University Press.

Oren, D. ([1985] 2001), *Joining the Club: A History of Jews at Yale*, 2nd edn, New Haven, CT: Yale University Press.

Orsi, R. ([1985] 2010), *The Madonna of 115th Street: Faith and Community in Italian Harlem, 1880–1950*, New Haven, CT: Yale University Press.

Ostwald, M. (2010), *Memoirs*. Available at: https://archive.org/details/ bib268016_001_001/ (accessed 8 July 2020).

Padilla Peralta, D. (2015), *Undocumented: A Dominican Boy's Odyssey from a Homeless Shelter to the Ivy League*, New York: Penguin.

Padilla Peralta, D. (2021), 'Anti-Race and Anti-Racism: Whiteness and the Classical Imagination', in D. McCoskey (ed.), *The Cultural History of Race, Volume One: A Cultural History of Race in Antiquity (500 BCE–800 CE)*, London: Bloomsbury.

Palmer, W. (2014), 'Carl Bridenbaugh, American Colonial History and Academic Anti-Semitism: The Paths to the "Great Mutation"', *American Jewish History*, 98: 153–74.

Pearce, S. (2007), 'Translating for Ptolemy: Patriotism and Politics in the Greek Pentateuch', in T. Rajak (ed.), *Jewish Perspectives on Hellenistic Rulers*, 165–81, Berkeley, CA: University of California Press.

Pelikan, J. (1996), *The Reformation of the Bible*: *The Bible of the Reformation*, New Haven, CT: Yale University Press.

Pelling, C. and S. Harrison, eds (2021), *Classics and Classicists: Essays on the History of Scholarship in Honour of Christopher Stray*, Berlin: De Gruyter.

Pemble, J., ed. (2000), *John Addington Symonds: Culture and the Demon Desire*, Basingstoke and London: Macmillan.

Perlman, J. (2018), *America Classifies the Immigrants: From Ellis Island to the 2020 Census*, Cambridge, MA: Harvard University Press.

Perry, S. (2021), 'Whitewashing Evangelical Scripture: The Case of Slavery and Antisemitism in the English Standard Version', *Journal of the American Academy of Religion*, 89: 612–43.

Pfeiffer, R. (1968), *History of Classical Scholarship: From the Beginnings to the End of the Hellenistic Age*, Oxford: Oxford University Press.

Pfeiffer, R. (1976), *History of Classical Scholarship, 1300–1850*, Oxford: Oxford University Press.

Phillips, A. (2014), *Becoming Freud: The Making of a Psychoanalyst*, New Haven, CT: Yale University Press.

Porter, A. (2004), *Religion versus Empire? British Protestant Missionaries and Overseas Expansion, 1700–1914*, Manchester: Manchester University Press.

Porter, J. (2008), 'Erich Auerbach and the Judaizing of Philology', *Critical Inquiry*, 35: 115–47.

Porter, J. (2010), 'Auerbach, Homer and the Jews', in S. A. Stephens and P. Vasunia (eds), *Classics and National Cultures*, 235–57, Oxford: Oxford University Press.

Porter, J. (2015), 'Jacob Bernays and the Catharsis of Modernity', in J. Billings and M. Leonard (eds), *Tragedy and the Idea of Modernity*, 15–41, Oxford: Oxford University Press.

Porter, J. (2017), 'Philology in Exile: Adorno, Auerbach and Klemperer', in H. Roche and K. Demetriou (eds), *Brill's Companion to the Classics, Fascist Italy and Nazi Germany*, 106–32, Leiden: Brill.

The Postclassicisms Collective (2019), *Postclassicisms*, Chicago, IL: University of Chicago Press.

Prins, Y. (1999), *Victorian Sappho*, Princeton, NJ: Princeton University Press.

Prins, Y. (2017), *Ladies' Greek: Victorian Translations of Greek Tragedy*, Princeton, NJ: Princeton University Press.

Pusey, E. (1854), *Collegiate and Professorial Teaching and Discipline in Answer to Professor Vaughan's Strictures*, Oxford and London: John Henry Parker.

Pym A. (2014), *Exploring Translation Theories*, London: Routledge.

Rajak, T. (2009), *Translation and Survival: The Greek Bible of the Ancient Jewish Diaspora*, Oxford: Oxford University Press.

Rajak, T., S. Pearce, J. Aitken and J. Dines, eds (2007), *Jewish Perspectives on Hellenistic Rulers*, Berkeley, CA: University of California Press.

Rankine, C. (2015), *Citizen: An American Lyric*, New York and London: Penguin.

Rankine, P. D. (2006), *Ulysses in Black: Ralph Ellison, Classicism, and African American Literature*, Madison, WI: University of Wisconsin Press.

Rankine, P. D. (2013), *Aristotle and Black Drama: A Theater of Civil Disobedience*, Waco, TX: Baylor University Press.

Rapple, B. (2017), *Matthew Arnold and English Education: The Poet's Pioneering Advocacy of Middle Class Instruction*, Jefferson, NC: McFarland.

Reinhartz, A. (2001), *Befriending the Beloved Disciple: A Jewish Reading of the Gospel of John*, New York and London: Continuum.

Reinhartz, A. (2018), *Cast Out of the Covenant: Jews and Anti-Judaism in the Gospel of John*, Lanham, MD: Lexington Books/Fortress Academic.

Ribeyrol, C. (2018), 'From Galatea to Tanagra: Victorian Translations of the Controversial Colours of Greek Sculpture', in K. Harloe, N. Momigliano and A. Farnoux (eds), *Hellenomania*, 179–93, Abingdon: Routledge.

Richardson, E. (2013), *Classical Victorians: Scholars, Scoundrels and Generals in Pursuit of Antiquity*, Cambridge: Cambridge Unniversity Press.

Roche, H. (2019), 'Mussolini's "Third Rome", Hitler's Third Reich and the Allure of Antiquity: Classicizing Chronopolitics as a Remedy for Unstable National Identity', *Fascism*, 8: 127–52.

Roche, H. and K. Demetriou, eds (2017), *Brill's Companion to the Classics, Fascist Italy and Nazi Germany*, Leiden: Brill.

Roedigger, D. (2005), *Working towards Whiteness: How America's Immigrants Became White: The Strange Journey form Ellis Island to the Suburbs*, New York: Basic Books.

Ronnick, M. (2000), 'William Sanders Scarborough: The First African American Member of the Modern Language Association', *PMLA*, 115: 1787–96.

Ronnick, M. (2011), 'Black Classicism: "Tell Them We are A-Rising"', *Classical Journal*, 106: 359–70.

Ronnick, M., ed. (2005), *The Autobiography of William Sanders Scarborough: from Slavery to Scholarship*, Detroit, MI: Wayne State University Press.

Ruden, S. (2021), *The Gospels*, New York: Modern Library.

Salaymeh, L. and S. Lavi (2021), 'Secularism', in S. Goldberg, S. Ury and K. Weiser (eds), *Key Concepts in the Study of Antisemitism*, 257–72, London: Palgrave Macmillan.

Sandwell, I. (2011), *Religious Identity in Late Antiquity: Greeks, Jews, and Christians in Antioch*, Cambridge: Cambridge University Press.

Satia, P. (2020), *Time's Monster: How History Makes History*, Cambridge, MA: Harvard University Press.

Saunders, M. (2010), *Self Impression: Life-Writing, Autobiografiction, and the Forms of Modern Literature*, Oxford: Oxford University Press.

Schäfer, P. (2009), *Judeophobia: Attitudes towards the Jews in the Ancient World*, Princeton, NJ: Princeton University Press.

Schwartz, S. R. (2013), 'Finkelstein the Orientalist', in W. V. Harris (ed.), *Moses Finley and Politics*, Columbia Studies in the Classical Tradition, Vol. 40, 31–48, Leiden and New York: Brill, and The Trustees of Columbia University in the City of New York.

Scott, J. W. (2018), *Sex and Secularism*, Princeton, NJ: Princeton University Press.

Ščrbačić, M. (2013), 'Von der Semitistik zur Islamwissenschaft und zuruck – Paul Kraus (1904–44)', *Simon Dubnow Institute Yearbook*, 12: 389–416.

Sellar, W. (1867), 'Theories of Classical Education: Lecture Delivered in Opening the Third Humanity Class, Friday November 8th, 1867', Edinburgh: Edmonston and Douglas.

Shavit, Y. (1997), *Athens in Jerusalem: Classical Antiquity and Hellenism in the Making of the Modern Secular Jew*, trans. C. Naor and N. Werner, London and Portland, OR: Littman Library of Jewish Civilization.

Sheehan, J. (2005), *The Enlightenment Bible: Translation, Scholarship, Culture*, Princeton, NJ: Princeton University Press.

Shteyngart, G. (2014), *Little Failure, A Memoir*, London: Penguin.

Shuger, D. (1994), *The Renaissance Bible: Scholarship, Sacrifice and Subjectivity*, Berkeley, CA: University of California Press.

Sidgwick, H. (1867), 'Theories of Classical Education', in F. W. Farrar (ed.), 81–144, London: Macmillan.

Simon-Nahum, P. (2005), 'Penser le judaïsme: Retour sur les Colloques des intellectuels juifs de langue français (1957–2000)', *Archives Juives*, 38: 79–106.

Simon-Nahum, P. (2010), 'Juif dans l'insoummission: La place du judaïsme dans les lectures de Jean Bollack', in C. König and D. Thouard (eds), *La Philologie au présent: Pour Jean Bollack*, 157–72, Villeneuve-d'Ascq: Presse universitaires du Septentrion.

Simon-Nahum, P. (2014), 'P. Vidal-Naquet-J. Bollack: Reflections around Two Readings of Tradition', *Cities*, 59: 163–7.

Snowden, F. (1970), *Blacks in Antiquity: Ethiopians in the Greco-Roman Experience*, Cambridge, MA: Harvard University Press.

Snowden, F. (1983), *Before Color Prejudice: The Ancient View of Blacks*, Cambridge, MA: Harvard University Press.

Snowman, D. (2002), *The Hitler Émigrés: The Cultural Impact on Britain of Refugees from Nazism*, London: Pimlico.

Stanley, B. (1990), *The Bible and the Flag: Protestant Missions and British Imperialism in the Nineteenth and Twentieth Centuries*, Leicester: Apollos.

Steiner, G. (1975), *After Babel: Aspects of Language and Translation*, Oxford: Oxford University Press.

Steiner, W. (1996), *The Scandal of Pleasure: Art in an Age of Fundamentalism*, Chicago, IL: University of Chicago Press.

Stephen, J.K. (1891), *The Living Languages: A Defence of the Compulsory Study of Greek at Cambridge*, Cambridge: Macmillan and Bowes.

Stephens, S. and P. Vasunia, eds (2010), *Classics and National Cultures*, Oxford: Oxford University Press.

Stille, A. (1991), *Benevolence and Betrayal*, New York: Summit Books.

Stow, K. (2006), *Jewish Dogs: An Image and Its Interpreters*, Stanford, CA: Stanford University Press.

Strauss Clay, J. (2003), 'The Real Leo Strauss', *New York Times*, June 7.

Stray, C. (1998), *Classics, Transformed: Schools, Universities and Society in England, 1830–1960*, Oxford: Oxford University Press.

Stray, C. (2014), 'Eduard Fraenkel: An Exploration', *Syllecta Classica*, 25: 113–72.

Stray, C. (2015), 'Eduard Fraenkel (1888–1970)', in S. Crawford, K. Ulmschneider and J. Elsner (eds), *Ark of Civilization: Refugee Scholars and Oxford University*, 180–201, Oxford: Oxford University Press.

Stray, C. (2018), *Classics in Britain: Scholarship, Education and Publishing, 1800–2000*, Oxford: Oxford University Press.

Stray, C., ed. (1999), *Classics in 19th- and 20th-Century Cambridge: Curriculum, Culture and Community*, Cambridge: Cambridge Philological Society.

Stray, C., ed. (2007), *Gilbert Murray Reassessed: Hellenism, Theatre, and International Politics*, Oxford: Oxford University Press.

Stroumsa, G. G. (1996), 'From Anti-Judaism to Anti-Semitism in Early Christianity?', in O. Limor and G. G. Stroumsa (eds), *Contra Iudaeos: Ancient and Medieval Polemics between Christians and Jews*, 1–26, Tübingen: Mohr Siebeck.

Stroumsa, G. G. (2007), 'Arnaldo Momigliano and the History of Religions', in P. N. Miller (ed.), *Momigliano and Antiquarianism: Foundations of the Modern Cultural* Sciences, 286–311, Toronto: Toronto University Press.

Stroumsa, G. G. (2021), *The Idea of Semitic Monotheism: The Rise and Fall of a Scholarly Myth*, Oxford: Oxford University Press.

Swinburne, A. (1925–7), *The Complete Works of Algernon Charles Swinburne*, eds A. C. Swinburne, E. Gosse and T. J. Wise, 15 vols, London: W. Heinemann.

Tadmor, N. (2010), *The Social Universe of the English Bible: Scripture, Society and Culture in Early Modern England*, Cambridge: Cambridge University Press.

Taylor, C. (2007), *A Secular Age*, Cambridge, MA, and London: Belknap Press of Harvard University Press.

Tompkins, D. (2006), 'The World of Moses Finkelstein: The Year 1939 in M. I. Finley's Development as a Historian', in M. Meckler (ed.), *Classical Antiquity and the Politics of America*, 95–126, Waco, TX: Baylor University Press.

Tompkins, D. (2016), 'The Making of Moses Finley', in D. Jew, R. Osborne and M. Scott (eds), *M. I. Finley: An Ancient Historian and His Impact*, 13–30, Cambridge: Cambridge University Press.

Treitler, V. (2013), *The Ethnic Project: Translating Racial Fiction into Ethnic Fiction*, Stanford, CA: Stanford University Press.

Turner, F. (1981), *The Greek Heritage in Victorian Britain*, New Haven, CT: Yale University Press.

Turner, J. (2014), *Philology: The Forgotten Origins of Modern Humanities*, Princeton, NJ: Princeton University Press.

Tyrrell, R. Y. (1899), 'Review of *Cambridge Compositions, Greek and Latin*, edited by R. D. Archer-Hind and R. D. Hicks, Cambridge: Cambridge University Press, 1899', *Classical Review*, 13 (4): 227–30.

Usher, H. J. K., C. Black-Hawkins and G. Carrick (1981), *An Angel without Wings: The History of University College School 1830–1980*, ed. G. Page, London: University College School.

Van Veller, C. W. (2019), 'John Chrysostom and the Troubling Jewishness of Paul', in C. de Wet and W. Mayer (eds), *Revisioning John Chrysostom: New Approaches, New Perspectives*, 1–31, Leiden: Brill.

Vasunia, P. (2013), *The Classics and Colonial India*, Oxford: Oxford University Press.

Venuti, L. (1995), *The Translator's Invisibility: A History of Translation*, London and New York: Routledge.

Vidal-Naquet, P. (1995), *Mémoires: La Brisure et l'attente, 1930–1955*, Paris: Éditions du Seuil/La Découverte.

Vidal-Naquet, P. (1998), *Mémoires: Le Trouble et la lumière 1955–1998*, Paris: Éditions du Seuil/La Découverte.

Vidal-Naquet, P. (2004), *Le Choix de l'histoire*, Paris: Arléa.

Waddell, W. (1890), *Versions and Imitations in Greek and Latin*, Glasgow: James Maclehose and Sons.

Wallace, J. (1997), *Shelley and Greece: Rethinking Romantic Hellenism*, Houndmills: Palgrave.

Wasserstein, D. (2005), 'Refugee Classicists in Britain after 1930', *Scripta Classica Israelica*, 24: 229–47.

Watts, M. S. (1913), *G. F. Watts: The Annals of an Artist's Life*, New York: Hodder and Stoughton.

Weber, E., ed. (1996), *Questions au judaïsme: Entretiens avec Elisabeth Weber*, Paris: Desclée de Brouwer.

Wideman, J. E. (1984), *Brothers and Keepers*, New York: Holt, Rinehart and Winston.

Wiese, C. and M. Thulin, eds (2021), *Wissenschaft des Judentums in Europe: Comparative and Transnational Perspectives*, Berlin and New York: De Gruyter.

Wilamowitz-Moellendorf, U. von (1982), *History of Classical Scholarship*, trans A. Harris, ed. with introduction and notes by Hugh Lloyd-Jones, Baltimore, MD: Johns Hopkins University Press.

Wilder, C. (2013), *Ebony and Ivy: Race, Slavery and the Troubled History of America's Universities*, New York: Bloomsbury.

Wilken, R. L. (1983), *John Chrysostom and the Jews: Rhetoric and Reality in the Late 4th Century*, Eugene, OR: Wipf and Stock.

Williams, G. (1970), 'Eduard Fraenkel 1888–1970', *Proceedings of the British Academy*, 56: 415–42.

Williams, P. (1991), *Alchemy of Race and Rights: Diary of a Law Professor*, Cambridge, MA: Harvard University Press.

Wilson, E. (2017), *The Odyssey of Homer*, New York: W. W. Norton.

Winkler, J. (1990), *The Constraints of Desire: The Anthropology of Sex and Gender in Ancient Greece*, New York and London: Routledge.

Wood, A. (2009), *Lynching and Spectacle: Witnessing Racial Violence in America, 1890–1940*, Chapel Hill, NC: University of North Carolina Press.

Wordsworth, C. (1890), *Annals of My Early Life*, London: Longmans, Green.

Wright, A. (1882), *Versus Tennysonianos Franklini Cenotaphio Inscriptos*, Cambridge: Deighton, Bell.

Yerushalmi, Y. H. (1982), *Zakhor: Jewish History and Jewish Memory*, Seattle, WA, and London: University of Washington Press.

Young, R. J. C. (1990), *White Mythologies*, London: Routledge.

Zeitlin, F., D. Barbu and A. Kachuk (2019), 'Entretien avec Froma Zeitlin', *Asdiwal*, 14: 79–88.

Ziolkowski, J. (2010), 'Middle Ages', in C. W. Kallendorf (ed.), *A Companion to the Classical Tradition*, 17–29, Oxford: Wiley-Blackwell.

Zon, B. and B. Lightman, eds (2019), *Victorian Culture and the Origins of Disciplines*, London: Routledge.

Index

Sparta 71–2
Stephen, J. K. 100
stereotyping 48, 58, 67
Stoicism 62
Strauss, Leo 56
Stray, Christopher 12, 152–3
sungeneia 30
Sun, the 24
supersessionism 26
Swift, Jonathan 144
Swinburne, Algernon 101
Syme, Ronald 70
Symonds, John Addington
112–13
symphilology 153
Syrian refugees 4–5

Taplin, Oliver 87
Taylor, Charles 56
Tebbit, Norman 3
'Tebbit Test' 3
Tennyson, Alfred 124, 126–7,
132–3, 157
Thalmann, Rita 52
Thames and Hudson publishing 76
*The Wife of Pygmalion. A translation
from the Greek* (Watts) 101
'Three Jolly Post Boys' (Tyrrell) 118,
127
Three Sisters (Chekhov) 41–2
Thucydides 82, 147
Tom Brown at Oxford (Hughes) 86
Tom Brown's Schooldays (Hughes) 41,
98
Tompkins, Dan 77
Translatio 13
translation,
awkwardness 133–40
classical tradition 140–58
culture of 95–105
double vision 123–33

and Walter Benjamin 105–23,
120–1n.68
Traumdeutung (Artemidorus) 39
Tupper, Martin Farquhar 146
Turkish Army 30
Tyrrell, R. Y. 117–18

UNESCO 28
University College London 133
University College School 133
University of Washington 15
Usher, Dr 138

Vasunia, Phiroze 152–3
Vaughan, Charles John 112, 122
Venuti, Lawrence 123
Vidal-Naquet, Pierre 55, 68,
70–4, 79
Virgil 24–5, 99, 136, 146
Voss, Johann Heinrich 128

Wagner, Richard 52, 148–50
Washington, George 41, 154
Watts, G. F. 101–2
white supremacists 20–1
Wilde, Oscar 149
Williams, Gordon 66
Wilson, Emily 42, 104–5
Winkler, Jack 42
Wisdom of Solomon (Headlam) 117,
123
Woolf, Virginia 100, 123
Wordsworth, William 122

Yale University 90, 117
yellow stars 56
Yerushalmi, Yosef Hayim 73,
73n.58
Yom Kippur 28

Zeitlin, Froma 86–7